T0209142

Free Spirit

CHLOE DELK

WESTBOW
PRESS®
A DIVISION OF THOMAS NELSON
& ZONDERVAN

WestBow Press books may be ordered through booksellers or by contacting:

WestBow Press
A Division of Thomas Nelson & Zondervan
1663 Liberty Drive
Bloomington, IN 47403
www.westbowpress.com
1 (866) 928-1240

Scripture quotations taken from The Holy Bible, New International Version® NIV® Copyright © 1973 1978 1984 2011 by Biblica, Inc. TM. Used by permission. All rights reserved worldwide.

Scripture taken from The Message. Copyright © 1993, 1994, 1995, 1996, 2000, 2001, 2002. Used by permission of NavPress Publishing Group.

ISBN: 978-1-9736-9312-3 (sc)
ISBN: 978-1-9736-9311-6 (hc)
ISBN: 978-1-9736-9313-0 (e)

Library of Congress Control Number: 2020910762

Print information available on the last page.

WestBow Press rev. date: 6/16/2020

Thank you to my grandparents, parents, siblings, and all of the other angels that God used to surround me in prayer my entire life. And a special thank you to my husband, who has never judged me, who has always loved me, and who has been my biggest supporter from day one. You are my greatest gift—and you will always be my favorite miracle.

Thank you to Jordan Younger for designing the amazing cover of the book, and Elijah Obcemea and Melanie Foust for helping me review and edit the manuscript. Thank you to my husband, Trent Delk, Pastor Mark, Pastor Rachelle Francey, and all of Oceans Church for investing in me and encouraging me to write this book and share my story.

This mystery has been kept in the dark for a long time, but now it's out in the open. God wanted everyone, not just Jews, to know this rich and glorious secret inside and out, regardless of their background, regardless of their religious standing. The mystery in a nutshell is just this: Christ is in you, so therefore you can look forward to sharing in God's glory. It's that simple. That is the substance of our Message. We preach *Christ*, warning people not to add to the Message. We teach in a spirit of profound common sense so that we can bring each person to maturity. To be mature is to be basic. Christ! No more, no less. That's what I'm working so hard at day after day, year after year, doing my best with the energy God so generously gives me. (Colossians 1:26–29)

Contents

Preface

This book was written as a conversation based on my story, the idea of what our world claims to be freedom, all with an emphasis on bridging the communication gap between the LGBTQ community and the church. A lot going on, I know! This book is not meant to be a casual read; I hope instead that my thoughts stir up thoughts within your own mind on this subject. Most of us know someone, or maybe it's you, who is searching for freedom in all the wrong places, and/or dealing with homosexuality or gender-identity confusion.

So why are these topics the least spoken about topics within the church body?

Well, I'll tell you. The reason why homosexuality—and really sexuality as a whole—isn't being spoken about in the church is because people are either too scared to create controversy, or they have withheld the truth from people they love in an attempt to maintain relationship with them. Real love, however, understands the urgency of salvation, and is willing to risk temporary reputation to obtain it. We cannot put our fears, feelings, or our earthly relationships above God. It is vital that we understand the state of our world, the realities of sin, and that we have the ability to discuss these topics without getting into arguments.

There are so many wounds that have been caused by hateful Christians, and there are also many people who have been misled by Christians who have taken singular parts of the Bible out of context. It's time for a disruptive movement that gives people the tools to have real conversations in a loving way. I am not saying that we need to preach about heavy topics every Sunday, but we, as a church body, need to be firm in who God is and represent Him correctly so that we can fulfill His mission: to lead everyone into His presence on earth and for eternity.

For years, no one has wanted to talk about these topics because of a fear of controversy and rejection. That has created a divide between the world and the church. What do I mean by divide? I do not mean the concept of being set apart from the world. I mean the church has pushed away people because of certain sins, causing people to feel like they have to choose a side. God's heart and vision has never been about division. It is about unity. It is time to call everyone home! How do we do this while still prioritizing truth?

God brought me out of my old life so that I could help others come out of it as well. The purpose of miracles and blessings is not so that we can just sit with them and enjoy them. It is so we can use them to help others receive them as well. God called me to bring everyone into His arms in an unconventional way: exposing certain things about myself in order to reach a generation that is hungry for realness and freedom. He has definitely taken me out of my comfort zone with this book. I hope that it is only the start of a conversation and a movement. This is just the beginning.

Introduction

M y goal in life, ever since I was a child, was to be free from worry, judgment, hatred, authority, and fear. I wanted so badly to never have to feel pain and to never have to be hurt. I chased after what the world told me freedom looked like. What was that? Well, it was doing whatever I wanted, whenever I wanted, to make myself feel good and avoid disappointment and discouragement. The definition of freedom is literally to do whatever one wants without anyone stopping them or holding them back.

For me, seeking freedom started off as casual. When someone hurt me, I would turn to drugs or sex or slander to get a false sense of pride and contentment. For me, it seemed casual, but I did not know that it wasn't normal. Then it quickly escalated. What began as temporary satisfaction and avoidance turned into addictions that led down a dark and traumatizing path. By the age of thirteen, I was having sex. By the age of fifteen, I was smoking marijuana and drinking. By the age of seventeen, I was doing all of those things, in addition to harder drugs like cocaine and ecstasy. By the age of about eighteen, I was a promiscuous, drug-dealing, drug-addicted abuse victim. By the age of twenty, I was a lesbian.

So how did a young girl, from a Christ-centered, family end up so lost and so broken?

When I was young, I used to dress up as a boy. It may seem like a simple statement, but it was really a deep internal struggle. Psychologists would call what I dealt with *gender dysphoria*. I believed in my heart, soul, and mind that I should have been born a boy. I had no concept of how to be a girl. Femininity was far beyond my understanding. I dressed like a boy, talked like a boy, walked like a boy, sat like a boy, and acted like a boy. It was so bad that I could not even look in the mirror without feeling uncomfortable with my identity. I remember constantly holding my hair back to see what I would look like with a shaved head. As this was going on, I did not understand that my personality didn't equal my sexuality. I did not understand what I was feeling or how to process it.

We will dive into that much deeper, but for now, just know that this confusion about my identity ended up making me believe that the key to freedom was achievable by finding "my truth." What began at a young age transformed into a life where I was abused, confused, abandoned, and mistreated—mostly because of my lack of identity and self-worth. I never told anyone what I was dealing with because I feared rejection. On top of that, no one ever stopped to talk to me about what was going on. Everyone either ignored the obvious signs or tried to change me into someone I was not.

This book is my story. It is a story full of abuse, drug addiction, mental health illness, promiscuity, and homosexuality. My goal of sharing my story with you is to spread the message that God loves everyone—no matter who they are or where they are in life. Another goal is to begin to bridge the communication gap between the LGBTQ community and the church. I hope to stir within everyone who reads this, a desire to know God more, to love deeper, and to listen and communicate with others better.

Our generation is on a search for truth and freedom. I hope this book will start a movement to direct this generation onto the right path. I pray that understanding and communication will evolve and the heart of Jesus will prevail. I am going to expose my innermost thoughts and life events. I pray that as I do so, you have a personal encounter with the Spirit of God. May He refine you, teach you, guide you, and leave you in a state of awe and wonder. May you find everlasting joy and true freedom from a free gift, a free Spirit: the Holy Spirit.

Chapter 1

It is proven that childhood has serious effects on adulthood. I had a relatively normal upbringing. My family comes from a long line of Armenian immigrants, who moved here during the Armenian genocide. My great-grandparents built their American dream from the ground up. My grandparents started working and got married at a young age. They created amazing lives for my parents to grow up in, and all of their grandchildren have been able to reap the benefits of the seeds they sowed. In my entire family line, there has never been homosexuality, divorce, addiction, hate, or even premature death. Everyone has always loved God, loved one another, and worked hard to keep the family bond strong. So, as you can see, I was—and still am, if we are being honest—the black sheep of the family.

Manhattan Beach, California, is one of the most beautiful places in the world, and it is where my parents decided to plant and build a firm foundation for me and my siblings. I am the youngest—and by far the craziest—of three children. My two siblings and I grew up in a great household; there was minimal fighting, we went to church every Sunday, and my parents both loved us well. My mom is a dentist, and my dad is a commercial real estate advisor; both are self-employed and highly successful.

My parents are the most amazing, loving, selfless people I have ever known, but somewhere along the line, I still went off track. If only good parenting was enough to keep children on track. They started me off on the way that I should go—the way of the Lord— and thanks to their faithfulness and prayers, I made it into the Father's arms. It took a while, however, and unfortunately, most of my life and my poor decisions were far outside of their control.

There is no doubt that all of my family members struggle with sin and the pressures of the world on a daily basis, but growing up, I never saw it. The people around me were doctors, lawyers, investment bankers, and in other highly admired professions. Meanwhile, I had no desire to be any of those things. I believed there was pressure to be perfect—not because of what anyone said, but because I never saw any problems in their day-to-day lives. My internal dialogue had begun attacking me from an early age, but I felt too ashamed to ever tell anyone. I became the most extroverted person on the outside, but internally I had closed myself off. I quickly began putting up a front. I was the child who was bubbly, fun, and always laughing, but I never told anyone what I was dealing with. I did not let anyone into my heart. I blocked off a lot of very real emotions and disguised them with laughter. That was the beginning of what the rest of my childhood, and young adult life, would look like. I tried so hard to be perfect that the pressure completely crushed me, and I ended up the complete opposite.

I believed that everyone around me had it all together and that I was the only broken one. Satan and my mind fed me lie after lie, and I bought into them, creating more and more insecurities. I knew that I was hurting. I knew that my life did not make sense. I isolated myself and became the person who everyone knew, but no one *really* knew. I was the one who could be in a room, surrounded by people, and still feel lonely and empty inside. I began keeping everyone around me at arm's length, and if anyone got too close, I would push them away. I truly believed that if any of my family or friends knew the real me, they would never love me. I wish I had spoken up and trusted someone. My desire for connection was strong, but I was too insecure to obtain it.

Because of the presence of social media today, insecurity has become an even more prominent issue. Back then, all we had was Myspace. I remember the Top Friends list on everyone's page; how I constantly compared myself and felt insecure when I wasn't on my friends' pages. I can only imagine the kind of comparison that children are facing now with multiple social media platforms and apps that can filter out all types of blemishes. We are in a world starved of connection. We desperately need close relationships with people we trust, but the majority of our social interaction takes place within an app. It is a scary and sad thought. I didn't struggle much with social media influence, but it was present in my life. The greater struggle for me, was the desire to be perfect and hide myself from the world. I felt that my family and friends were all perfect—but I was not. This was obviously a lie, but I believed it subconsciously.

My problems were not external; all my problems were internal. Yes, bad things happened throughout my life, but they were not meant to wound me. My sister became extremely ill when we were children, and the effects only made my insecurities worse. For years, I watched my parents cater to her every need, and it left me feeling isolated and neglected. When I look back now, I am so glad that my parents loved my sister so well through that, but as a child, I had no idea what was going on.

Chapter 2

G rowing up, I was a tomboy. I dressed in my brother's clothes, while every girl around me was dressed in skirts and dresses and learning how to do their hair and put on makeup. I remember the first time I decided I would try to fit in. My mom bought me a blue velvet skirt. I wore it often, but it was horrible—not to mention extremely ugly.

My friend's mom had a clothing line, and she would have these trunk show things in her garage. I would always go, but I hated everything there. Meanwhile, my friends were all so excited to model all the apparel. It is comical that I can distinctly remember the only skirt that I ever bought or wore. Before that skirt, all I owned were boxers, cargo shorts, skater shoes, and those pants that have zippers at the knees so you can turn your pants into shorts. Yes, I know, fashion was never my strong suit; it was all about practicality. I loved to feel free in baggy clothing, and I loved the convenience of switching from pants to shorts so easily!

Unfortunately, when you are dressed like a boy, most boys are not interested in you. And you know how elementary school goes: children start crushing on one another. Girls and boys all around me were crushing on one another, but all I wanted was to be friends with the boys. Everyone loves a good elementary-school crush except for me, apparently.

People would always comment about my appearance, tell me that I was one of the boys, or tell me that I looked like a boy. In elementary school, my mom's friends would always tell me how they drove by the school and saw me playing basketball outside with all the guys. I blended right in with the boys. Honestly, I loved it. I wasn't interested in boys like some of my friends were. I just wanted to play basketball and hang out! There was nothing wrong with that, but I kept feeling like something about me must have been off.

I was one of the best video game players, I could skateboard and wakeboard like a professional, and I was a national all-star basketball player. My guy friends and I—as well as my best friend, who was a tomboy too—would go to my house after school and play video games, skateboard, and play street hockey. That was what my life looked like.

When I got older, I would travel for club basketball on weekends. I played for a few teams, and we traveled the country together, winning multiple nationals. I was an amazing point guard and shooting guard. I used to wear number 24, and my dad would call me "Klobe," after Kobe Bryant. I was the number one pick for basketball and softball; the dads used to fight over who would get me on their team. I was a pretty awesome athlete, and I had a lot going for me, but I threw it all away because of insecurity and shame.

When I was not hanging out with anyone, and no one was around at home, I would secretly put on television shows where the actors and actresses were living homosexual lifestyles because it was the only time when I felt like anyone understood me. I saw other girls dressed like boys, and when I saw them dating other girls, things started to come together in my head.

That is the influence that the media has over our lives. The church cannot allow the media to be our children's source of information on this topic.. At that time, there were very few shows like that, but somehow, I found them. That dark, spiritual, magnetic pull grew stronger and stronger. The enemy was winning—and I didn't even know I was in a spiritual war.

No one made me have same-sex attractions, and that is one argument many use to try to prove that people must be born homosexual. It had always been part of my life, from as early as I can remember, but it manifested at different times in different ways. I stand by the fact that my gender-identity struggle was real from a young age, and I don't attribute those thoughts or actions to any one person. However, I would like to bring attention to people's influences on my state of mind. It did not help to constantly hear people tell me that I looked like a boy. It did not help to constantly hear people tell me that I might be gay. We have to be careful about what we are feeding young children. We can shape a child's direction, with prayer and what we speak. We need to speak life over them because the power of the tongue is real.

While it was all true, I did not need to hear people planting ideas and thoughts in my head at such a young age. Just because I struggled with my femininity—and just because I was an all-star tomboy—does not mean that I was a boy. So what gave people the right to go and speak those kinds of things over an innocent child? Why does our society link personality and sexuality? If only someone had come to me back then and helped me talk through all my confusion. Communication can change the world.

We have to be careful with our words. In a world where we are pushing for children as young as kindergarten to learn about different genders and sexual orientations, we need to speak up and stand up for innocence. Innocence is being stripped away from children. It was stripped away from me, and laws were not even passed to encourage it at the time. We need to understand that we are not helping when we force children to label themselves, or worse, put labels on them ourselves.

Is that really freedom? I would argue that we are actually ensalving children to gender and sex by subjecting them to certain labels at such a young age. We need to allow them to express themselves as children without forcing them into decisions that will falsely affect the rest of their lives. Just because a child has a strong personality does not mean that we should change their God-given gender. Their personality does not dictate their sexuality.

Labeling yourself or someone else as gay, lesbian, transgender, or bigender—you get the idea—is actually dehumanizing. I am speaking about this from experience, in love. The enemy convinced me and has convinced many other people that subjecting yourself to a label is becoming free and true to yourself. In reality, you are so much more than your sexual orientation or gender. It is almost like the label is all that you are or all that you were made for, which seems like a limited life to me. Satan doesn't want anyone to see that he is actually calling them by their sin. He is a master of disguising darkness, and making it appear to be beautiful, but it is not. Satan sees you for your sin and darkness; God sees you for your beauty and purpose. Choose to listen to God.

I am against labeling in general, but specifically in this area, because God never meant for us to identify with sin:

> For the sexually immoral, for those practicing homosexuality, for slave traders and liars and perjurers—and for whatever else is contrary to the sound doctrine. (1 Timothy 1:10 NIV)

In the Bible, homosexuality was not used as a noun or an adjective; it was used as a verb, an action. Humans created the LGBTQ community labels, making an identity out of a behavior. It has become a permanent label, where people argue that it is something that they cannot change. However, my question is: if straight people can become gay, why can't gay people become straight? This might be new to you, so hear me out: God does not call us or know us by our sinful actions. He loves us as His children. For example, when Jesus approaches a prostitute, He does not call her a prostitute. He forgives her and tells her to move forward. Satan is the one who wants to label you by your sin. God wants to label you as a holy, anointed son or daughter. God calls us by our name and not by our pain. Be careful with the words and names you use because they hold much more importance than we like to admit.

I wish that, as a child, someone told me that God saw me for much more than what I could see and feel. That is why it is important that we learn how to have discussions about sexual sin with children today. We need to appropriately discuss who God designed us to be and what that should look like in our lives. We need to explain that Jesus doesn't label sin; He redeems it. He died to cover it. We need to fight the stripping of our children's innocence with the power of the truth.

Contemplate this for a minute. No one says, "I'm a thief. That's just me. It's who I am." They don't walk around every day and flaunt it. No one's Instagram bio says, "I'm a porn addict. It's who I am. I love to masturbate." That is not how they view themselves; they view themselves as more than their sin. So what is so different about homosexuality? Why is it that it is the one sin that generates labels and has our entire society in a major global identity crisis?

Have you ever wondered why the LGBTQ community has their Pride events? Let me tell you, as someone who used to attend them, the pride comes from the fact that most everyone with same-sex attractions or gender-identity confusion has dealt with abandonment, abuse, rejection, and hate. It is fun at the events, of course, but it is not just about the fun. It is a celebration of overcoming injustice.

The labels used in the LGBTQ community are worn and idolized because the human race never operated out of love and understanding; it operated out of judgment and abuse. How can we work together to bridge this gap? The old churches pushed people dealing with homosexuality so far away that it became an issue about LGBTQ versus the church. God never separated Himself from sinners. How do we learn, understand, and communicate? How do we resolve this divide like Jesus would want us to?

> Or do you not know that wrongdoers will not
> inherit the kingdom of God? Do not be deceived:

Neither the sexually immoral nor idolaters nor adulterers nor men who have sex with men nor thieves nor the greedy nor drunkards nor slanderers nor swindlers will inherit the kingdom of God. And that is what some of you were. But you were washed, you were sanctified, you were justified in the name of the Lord Jesus Christ and by the Spirit of our God. (1 Corinthians 6:9–11 NIV)

You see, before God, we are known for our sin. Once we are sanctified, we are seen as God sees us: justified and holy! God did not refer to one as worse than another. All the sins listed above are all equally sinful in God's eyes. If we could see homosexuality as a sin, equal to any other sin in the Bible, maybe then we could love those in it as Jesus does.

Honestly, we could have avoided a lot of what we are going through today if we had. Who are we as people to decide who's allowed to stay in the church and who has to leave? Who are we to decide who gets to hear about the Gospel and who doesn't? Who are we to decide who is too far gone or who can still change? We have no power in this area; all of the power is in the hands of Jesus. The truth is that we do not know anything. We have no idea what God's plan is, who He wants to speak to, and how it is going to happen. So, let's stop playing God. Instead, let's allow God to use us in whatever way He wants, with whomever He wants, however He wants.

Because there was so much bottled up inside, when I came out, it was like the ultimate sense of freedom. Looking back, it was not freedom, but it resembled the feeling. I realized that I no longer had to pretend. I no longer had to fear. I no longer had to hide in the dark without community. Wearing the label "bisexual" and then eventually "homosexual", felt freeing because it seemed to sum up all of my internal feelings and battles. It was as if the label itself wore my shame and fear instead of me. Sound familiar?

You see, Satan has closely linked the same feeling as accepting Jesus and knowing the Holy Spirit with "coming out of the closet" and becoming who you truly are. Really think about how strategic and how good Satan is at manipulating people into believing that "their own truth" will set them free. There is only one Truth that will set you free, and that is Jesus Christ, the Way, the Truth, and the Life. Jesus alone bore our sin and shame, no label, person or movement can do that.

What a word for today! An entire generation is growing up being told to "find their own truth." Our world is being operated by the idea that freedom means putting yourself before anyone else. This breaks my heart, and it hits way too close to home. I lived this lie, and I hurt everyone around me, including myself.

The Word of God needs to be preached now, louder than ever. Truth has to be spoken, and stories need to be told. All too often, we hear stories of people on the side of darkness, while people in the church are hiding because they do not think they need to share hope! We need to be "salt in light." We cannot sit back and let people believe the stories of false hope our culture has immersed them in. They are being suffocated and surrounded by lies, but they have no knowledge of what is true. There is such a big gap! We need to communicate Jesus to this world.

Chapter 3

B efore I jump into the next stage of my life, I want to mention that I grew up going to church every Sunday with my family. However, the church never stuck with me. From drawing pictures of Noah and Jonah every Sunday to having weird conversations with adults, I just never liked Sunday school. I was always the child trying to sit in the main service with her parents, avoid Sunday school, and just draw on the church handouts for an hour.

When I was in fifth grade, one of the small group leaders in Sunday school specifically asked the young girls in my group who in the group thought they were going to remain a virgin until they were married. That is a weird thing to ask children, right? For me, as a child who was around other children acting like we were way older than we were, the question started a whole conversation in my head. I distinctly recall that everyone raised their hand except me—and that was the moment I started feeling like I was not godly. I started feeling like I was not enough. After that, I really didn't like church, and I had no interest in going. You can see the irony in the fact that God has now called me into full-time children's ministry. God is so funny.

I got really turned off to church when it felt like everything that was expected, I just could not do. I felt like it was just rules and regulations and that I wasn't actually going to get to live a free life. I wanted freedom, and if I wasn't going to find that in the church, then my solution was to leave the church. I believe that if we are going to call back a generation of people who left the church—or who do not know anything good or correct about the church—then we need to stand up for what the truth really is. The truth is that God does not take things away from us by force. It is not about what we are losing or what we can't do. We need to focus on what we gain. Stop focusing on what we lose when following Jesus, when there is so much more that we gain. There is such a need for the church to be sharing the good news about Jesus. We need to make it known that there is so much more to life that we access through Jesus Christ than anything that the world has to offer. Freedom, love, joy, peace, and contentment—all of the ultimate gifts that this world is looking for—are all found in Jesus.

Why are we focusing on what people can't do or everything that people have to give up, when we could be focusing on everything that the person would gain by following Jesus Christ? Churches, speaking the truth is important, but I believe that also focusing on the miracles and wonders of God will help people not leave the church. So many people are leaving the church because they are not understanding the goodness and fullness of God. We just need to approach it with order. The first step is leading people into the presence of God, and once they are there, letting God do His work in them at His appointed time! Once the questions start coming, and the transfiguration starts happening, that is when we need to be there, Word of God in hand, ready to comfort, edify, and encourage!

I rebelled against the church because I felt limited, but when you follow Jesus, you are unlimited; you have unlimited access to God, the source of life. You even have unlimited authority over the world! Since I did not understand this key concept, after elementary school, I entered into a pivotal moment of my childhood. That is a common time for people to have major identity crises. I really never knew myself, and I suppressed all of my gender confusion and mental health struggles. For a little while, my life took on other struggles like drug addiction and abusive relationships. I had already been confused about church, and right after that moment in my small group, I started feeling like I was not right for church at all. I don't think my leader thought anything of it since we were just children, but it stuck with me. My mind was much more mature than she thought. I believed that I was not welcome there and that it wasn't for me. Shortly after that, I decided to leave the church because I did not want to keep going.

This lack of fitting in and a lack of self-awareness caused me to turn to tangible coping mechanisms. I used sex and drugs to hide my internal struggles. The first time I touched a drug was when I was in sixth grade. I was already engaging in sexual activities and drinking, but I remember the first time I smoked marijuana. Someone brought weed to a usual hangout spot, but of course, there was nothing to smoke it with. So I got a can and poked holes in it. Real luxurious, right? Nothing really happened that night—I did not actually feel any high—but it was a gateway to being willing to smoke and do other drugs. I was not afraid of drugs anymore; the door had been opened.

As my body, soul, and mind attacked one other on a daily

basis, my physical appearance and personality showed none of it. I was the queen of faking, or at least I thought I was. For my entire life, I looked like I had it all together, mainly because I convinced myself that I did! I dated guys, slept with guys, and tried to dress like a girl as best as I could. I did everything to appear like my life was so good, but deep down, I hated all of it. Honestly, I did not even like to party; I just felt the pressure to fit in. It was the only time that I felt like I was worth anything to anyone.

I was really good at making people believe I was confident and put together. I just wanted people to like me and not reject me. It is a nice thought—until you realize that striving to be someone in order to please other people actually costs you your own soul. On a search for freedom, I lost myself, more than I even thought was possible. My life was a big oxymoron. Is freedom really becoming someone you were never meant to be? I kept sinking deeper and deeper. It is crazy that it was not possible for me to see it until I saw myself as Jesus does. At the time, I would not have been able to see how lost I was. I really thought I had it all figured out, but now, it is so clear to me how confused I was.

I couldn't see how lost I was because I was on drugs, and drugs give you an out-of-body experience. Drugs bring out false ideas and feelings. I felt like I could see the world as God designed it to be. What do I mean? Let me clarify. The highs that I got from certain drugs made me see the world in a perfect light. The best way that I can explain it is like you're in this euphoric state of mind where nothing is wrong, nothing is broken, and everything is beautiful and perfect! Think about the way you see colors every day, and then think about what those colors look like if you magnified the saturation by one hundred. And, so, of course people get addicted to drugs. You take a broken person, born into a broken world, and you put them on a high that seems like it is perfect. It is not a wonder why I never wanted to come down. That is why drugs should never be taken, unless used for medical needs and monitored by doctors, because doors like this are much better off left unopened.

I was trying to find freedom and find myself. In middle school, I made friends with some really popular, cool kids. They were the beautiful rich kids of Manhattan Beach, in Southern California, who everyone wanted to be like at the time. I thought that since I made it into that group, I had made it in life! I mean, who doesn't want to be cool? My friends were awesome, and I am still friends with most of them. However, we got into a lot of bad things at a really young age. I was about twelve when my life started turning upside down. I was living like I was forty years old. I was doing things that no thirteen-year-old should ever do, but at the time, it just seemed so normal to me. I felt alone and confused, and I was finding friends who had what I wanted at the time. That seemed to make the most sense.

By about seventh grade, I was smoking weed, drinking alcohol, and having sex. You see, smoking and drinking numbed me, and having sex with boys made me feel like I was a "normal" girl, even though I did not like it. I created a pattern of meaningless sex just to be able to fit in and feel attention from someone else. It was not enjoyable, but it offered me a fake sense of security. I soon started feeling empty, and I quickly started trying to keep filling myself with more and more. For some reason, I just kept getting rejected. Let's be real. No one wants to be around a hurting person. I was the only one who could not see that I was hurting.

I never understood why people were rejecting me, and that drove me to even more insecurities. It was a real bottomless pit.

A lot of my friends who were girls constantly made fun of me because I was not like them, but I never tried to find new friends because I was desperate. I just stayed close to the few who did not judge me. The rest did not know what they were doing, but it hurt. Even though I ignored it, I felt it deeply. All my friends who were boys, I was allowing to sleep with me, but once they were done with me, they moved on and began dating my best friends. I was not who anyone wanted—or at least that was how it all made me feel.

I had entered into a new level of life. I turned into a really bad person, but I used the excuse that I was a good person. I even think that I often called myself a Christian. I have always been someone who likes to help people. I love people. I was really nice, I was very popular, and I really believed that I was a good person—even though I was basically just trying to find satisfaction at the expense of everyone else's. After growing up in the church, I thought the label of Christian was just a part of life. I never understood that it is life, all of life. I tried to make myself happy by hurting other people even though I claimed that I wasn't hurting anyone. I didn't view it that way, but that's really what it was at the end of the day. As they say, "Hurt people hurt people."

I want to take this moment to focus on how I called myself a Christian. For a while, I was tossing around the word *Christian* without even knowing what it really meant. Too often, people are just like me in this instance. We have been calling ourselves Christians without actually living with Christ. It is an immediate turnoff to many around us because they see the wrong image and representation of Jesus.

If you have been like this too, or are like this right now, I have good news for you. God is bigger than you, and He already forgives you! Turn to Jesus, face Him, and let Him show you what walking with the Holy Spirit really looks like! I find rest in the concept that He is so big that He can repair any damage that I caused by leading people astray. Everyone who I might have accidentally driven away from Christ is not done for because God can use any mistake and any wrongdoing for good! He really does work all things together for good!

Chapter 4

M iddle school was quite the adventure, but it was just the start. High school was where it went up another level. During high school, I really lost myself. It just kept getting worse. Even though I thought I was becoming freer in life, I was actually getting more lost. I was a great basketball player, I was smart, and I was super popular. I managed to be under the influence 24/7 and still pass all my classes. I had one of the strongest families ever and all the support in the world. I had a ton of friends as well, but they only liked hanging out with me when I was throwing my life away. Funny how we always think those are our true friends, right? They support you when you are doing bad things, but they leave your side when you try to improve yourself. I'm pretty sure they all think I am nuts now that I follow Jesus and don't do the things I used to do.

As I got closer to my friends, I started to throw everything else away, especially my family. I began pushing and pushing. I was addicted to drugs, and if I wasn't able to do drugs when I was with my family, I would go through withdrawal. I would be angry, impatient, and crazy! It destroyed my relationships with them. I began spewing hateful words constantly. I regrettably told my parents countless times that I hated them and wished they were dead. I used to physically fight my sister and verbally attack her. While this is hard for me to admit even now, seeing as God has fully restored my relationships with my family, it is a testament to His faithfulness and redemptive nature. God wants to restore our relationships and use them to give hope to others who have broken relationships that seem impossible to mend.

I wish that it stopped at my relationships with my family, but it didn't. I was ruining all the relationships around me, including intimate relationships and friendships. For most of high school, I was dating a good-looking, super nice guy. He was ASB president and a volleyball player, but I found myself cheating on him constantly and treating him like garbage. At the time, I thought it was all his fault, and that was the beginning of a bad pattern.

My boyfriend was a "straight edge" at the time, but he was dating a hippie-druggie girl, and you can see where things were going wrong for us. I was like a chameleon though. I had so many different identities, and I was constantly changing to adapt to my surroundings. I was one person one minute and someone else the next. He did his best to keep up. I give him credit. On prom night, we had an after-party. All my friends and I were doing hard drugs, and my boyfriend found out and avoided me the whole night. You would think that I would have learned how that upset him and maybe stop, but freedom to me was doing whatever I wanted without anyone else holding me back. There was no stopping me.

My friends and I would go to Cancun for spring break every year. I am pretty sure I literally had a fake ID to say that I was eighteen years old because we were not even allowed to drink in Mexico because we were so young. We were all drinking by the hotel pool one day, and I ended up getting roofied. I blacked out and came to on a lawn chair by the pool. I felt off, and I knew something was wrong. I crawled back to the hotel room on all fours, barely making it to the door.

God had His hand over me because it ended up being that one of my friends hadn't left the room yet. When she heard me, she brought me inside. I stayed in bed, sleeping, throwing up endlessly, and screaming random words. Something like that might shock some people, but my friends videotaped me—and we all watched it for months after that cracking up. I had just blocked myself off from so much that I literally could've had something horrible happen to me, and I just did not care. I thought it was funny.

More traumatic events happened during high school, but my brain has done a good job of blocking them out. I sometimes get flashbacks or remember certain things, and it breaks my heart and really scares me. Bad things happened, based on poor decisions, like taking my friend's mom's car out at night when I didn't have a license yet. We got pulled over, but luckily nothing bad happened. I did crazy, not smart things that I cannot even identify with now. I do not even understand how I did those things. I was so careless and selfish. I am so thankful for God's provision over my life—even when I did not know He was there.

Fast-forward to the grad night at the end of high school. My boyfriend and I had made it through a lot of my mistakes. I normally would break up with him so that I could feel better about myself dating other guys at the same time. It was twisted, I know, and I am not proud of it. Actually, I am disgusted by my actions. I was so sad that I could treat another human being the way I treated him. However, God forgave me. I have learned to forgive myself and not live in the past!

On the bus to grad night, I had taken ecstasy. I began entering a euphoric state and acting like the bus was a rocket ship. He quickly figured out that I was using drugs all of the time, and I am pretty sure that night was a big turning point for him. He had too much self-respect to continue to date me. As the summer before college began, we ended up calling it quits so we could move on and embrace college on our own. There were moments during the first year of college that we tried to date, like everyone who goes to college with a high school relationship, but it was short-lived.

Before college, I went on a vacation with some friends. It is one of the most distinct adventures that I remember of those lighthearted, carefree, free-spirited days. We began our ten-hour drive up the coast in my old jeep. We decided to go camping, hang out, and take acid on the beach. Once we were settled in at our little campground on the beach, we dropped our acid and started our way toward the beach. We were climbing over rocks and having a great time. We were on an extreme high. It was a feeling I can't explain without just saying that it felt like perfect freedom.

Two of my friends and I were swimming in the ocean, fully clothed and basking in what felt like heaven on earth. As we decided to head back, we noticed that one of my friends never made it to the ocean. Nothing bad happened to her, thank God, but my friend was standing in a sewage drainage area in the sand. At first, we looked at her and saw how big her smile was. As we approached, we found that she was standing by a huge dead bird and a bunch of trash. We realized she was not in the ocean; she was in a sewage-filled hole in the sand.

I love what a metaphor that story really is. The world is telling us that we are standing in the ocean. We have been acting like it is total freedom, and we believe that we are standing in beauty. In reality, we are dancing in a sewage drain in front of the ocean. We don't even understand that we haven't even actually made it to the ocean because we are so caught up in the things of this world. We are raised to be caught up in instant gratification and instant satisfaction, and we end up caught in the sewage before we reach the ocean. How unfortunate! We are not even in the beautiful waters yet, but we're believing a lie and telling ourselves that this is as good as it's going to get. That life without Jesus, truly is beautiful. Truth is beautiful. In reality, we're standing in a dump and believing the lie. In essence, we are depriving ourselves of ever making it into the ocean.

So many people around me have said that God hasn't healed them or helped them; therefore, they continue to sin. God will always heal us and remove our sins; we just have to take them seriously and want them gone. People try to surrender to God, but a part of them still wants to hold on to their sins and past life. They see the ocean ahead, but they can't quite let go of the sewage behind them. This is particularly true for homosexuality. This is why people believe it is not just a sin. They believe it is something that people cannot change at all. Truthfully, speaking from experience, since sexual immorality just feels so right and so freeing, part of us is not ready to let go when God calls us to. Then we give up, claiming that God does not have anything better for us, and we become enslaved to sin.

I encourage you to get out of the sewage. Can I propose that there's a beautiful ocean waiting for you on the other side? The

Spirit of God is waiting for you to come into His arms so that he can surround you, hold you, dance with you, and love you. You don't need to be in the sewage any longer.

We don't even know what true beauty is because we are so distracted by fake beauty like drugs, sex, social media, alcohol, and other idols. We don't even know what God has because we are not the Creator of this world, but we think we're all-knowing. We think we know what's right and what's wrong. We think we know what's the best for us and everyone around us, and we convince ourselves that it's never going to get better. Could it be that we are just too scared to give God a chance? Why can't we entertain the thought that there might be something better for us? Are we too scared to put down everything that we have placed our hopes in? In reality, placing our hope in other people, who are just as temporary as we are, or things that are not even alive, like homes and cars, will never give us everlasting and fulfilling hope. And could this be why we are such a depressed and anxious generation?

I know I was scared. I thought I had it all. I thought I did not need God. I could kind of see the ocean in the distance, but it was not worth it for me.

Chapter 5

I went to Santa Barbara to visit friends right before college, and something bad happened. I was being my normal self, drunk and having a good time, and then the rest became a blur. I got roofied again. When I came to, I found myself being taken advantage of by a random college guy in the back of a car on the side of the street. That was the first time a part of me that I could never get back was taken like that; unfortunately, it was not the last. This is the hardest part for me to write. I can see why it led me into college even worse than expected. When it happened to me, I felt guilt, shame, and more worthlessness than I could handle. I put so much blame on myself and went to what I knew best: numbing myself.

I became heavily addicted to drugs by the end of high school, and all of a sudden, it was time for me to go to college. My whole life, I did not care about education. I miraculously graduated from high school, but I had horrible grades and horrible SAT scores. I did not get accepted to many schools, but I did get accepted to the University of Colorado in Boulder. I was so excited about going to Boulder because I felt like I could really find my groove there. From what I could tell, everyone there was a free-spirited hippie, and they were all just living a fun life with no cares.

Once I got there, I immediately fell in love with the school. I mean, who wouldn't? It is one of the most beautiful campuses in the United States. It was my dream school. We could hang out, we could do drugs, and we could skip around on fields of grass, tripping out together and having the time of our lives. By that time, drugs were the norm for me. I was on a consistent high. In my mind, I was free, but I was actually a slave to drugs. I had to start taking even harder drugs and more drugs in order to actually feel high. Classical conditioning had caused my body to get used to the intake of drugs.

Second semester of my first year in Colorado, I was in a sorority. That was one of my tactics to try to have a life that I thought was cool and normal in order to hide that I was a mess. While living a heterosexual, promiscuous life, I ended up in a bad relationship. The relationship started out fun and casual, but did not end up that way. I was on so many drugs, and I actually became a drug dealer. I was shipping in drugs from other places and selling them to people at school. I honestly cannot recall much about that time of my life.

Unfortunately, at the time, I thought it was the best life ever. I thought I had it all. I thought I was dating someone I deserved because of the lies and fake feelings that drugs and sex were feeding me. I became severely underweight, lost most of my intimate friends, and pushed away my family even more. On top of that, my friends were dropping like flies all around me. It was a reoccurring thing to hear of friends who had overdosed or committed suicide, but none of it was enough to change the way I was living. Not even death could get me to try for a better life.

My life at that time consisted of parties, taking Xanax, and watching *Trailer Park Boys*. I was just wasting my life away, all at the age of about eighteen. I was losing friends to overdoses on the regular. People dying, or having near-death experiences, was extremely normally at that point. A random guy who I was dealing drugs with actually got arrested. I feared getting caught and ending up in jail as well.

I underwent a lot of abuse and stalking. I was dragged across streets and shoved into walls. I still have flashbacks of being attacked. If you are going through abuse right now, I want to tell you that you are so much more than that. Abuse is not okay. God sees you, He hears you, and He loves you. His heart will set you free and set you on a new path. You can get out of the situation that you might be stuck in—or thinking you deserve—like I did. You don't have to live like that any longer. You do not have to fear man. Please seek help if that is you; we have to fight against injustice.

Do not be afraid of this world and what others might think of you. Trust in Jesus. Find someone who believes in Jesus and confide in them. Have them pray with you, have them love you, and have them take care of you. Please make sure that you do this in a safe way.

At that moment, I did not actually understand what was going on or see the truth. However, once I was out of the relationship, it all became clear.

College went on and it was full of fun. I am not going to lie to you—sin is fun—but add a few letters, and *fun* turns into *funeral*. Do you get what I am saying? It was fun in the moment, but it was not freedom. My college days consisted of tailgating, partying, concerts, festivals, raves, and somehow managing to make it to class sometimes.

My scariest encounter was probably when I was on vacation with friends in Spain. I actually got lost at a beach club during the day. We were there all day and into the night. A guy tried to take me with him, and I needed a way to ditch him. I could not find my friends, and I had no money left. I managed to collect enough change to get on a bus, but I was so lost that I didn't know where I was going. I ended up not having enough change for the next bus. I was stranded in the middle of nowhere. I ended up, by myself, as a teenage girl, hitchhiking through the streets. Somehow, this car of actual nice guys found me and drove me back to my hotel. I will never forget how scared I was at that moment. However, the next day, I just forgot it even happened. Thank God for His provision over my life—even when I did not notice or receive it!

On the outside, my life looked like fun vacations, raves, festivals, friends, and money, but on the inside, everyone was so lost. I thought life was nothing more than being drunk, being high, and having no care for anything or anyone. From an outsider's perspective, we were just living the dream life. Everyone's Instagram pages looked great, but we all knew the truth. Like when you know your friends who are dating, are in the biggest fight, but then you see them post a photo of them kissing and smiling on Instagram. Or when someone who hates their job is at work all day and is posting pictures of them on vacation, making their life look glamorous. You get the point. My life looked perfect on the outside, but I began noticing just how ugly it actually was.

In the summer before junior year of college, I was at home

in Southern California. I finally started to notice that something was not right. One morning, after a hard week, I woke up with a new vision. I started seeing my life with a new perspective, but I couldn't put my finger on it. At first, it was too heavy for me to bear. I felt disgusted with myself. I felt regret. I felt shame. I felt embarrassed. I felt everything that I had suppressed for so long. I had acted like it wasn't there, but everything I had ever done came rushing over me. It was like sitting in a bus, and the back of the bus was filled to the brim with trash. All of a sudden, I stepped on the brakes—and all the trash came smashing in front of me. It was all I could see. I panicked. I did not know how to clean it all up while driving. I felt like it was time for me to just crash the bus.

It was too much for me to handle. I was so overwhelmed. It was the first time that I became severely suicidal. I didn't know who I was. I couldn't understand everything wrong I had done. I felt like there was no way out and nowhere to go from there. I decided to grab a knife from downstairs.

As I walked out of my room, my sister was standing in the middle of the hallway. My sister and I were the furthest thing from friends, yet God used her as my angel in that moment. I fell into her arms and just started crying and weeping. She said two phrases that changed my life: "This isn't you. You are more than this."

In that moment, hope came over me. I knew it was God. I went back into my room and just cried and started talking to a God I knew nothing about. I heard a thought so loud: "Chloe, this is not the end of your life—but a start of a new one." I kept crying. I did not know what God's voice actually sounded like, but I heard it and believed it. I decided to make some life changes.

I do not write these stories about my life to brag about them or sulk in them. Quite frankly, I wish many people who will read this book don't ever actually know what I have done or been a part of. Writing this book is breaking my heart. But in telling you, it is also reminding me of the goodness of God. Remembering what my life was like before Christ makes me so thankful that we have a God who loves us even though we do not deserve it.

Words cannot accurately describe how thankful I am or how hard these things are for me to write out on paper. I write these stories to you because I want to make a point. No matter what we have done—no matter how dirty we are—we are still chosen by God, and we are still loved. Nothing from our past defines our present or our future when we surrender our lives to Christ. We are made new. Praise the Lord! I do not live with guilt, embarrassment, shame, or resentment. I choose to use my past to change the future.

I wish I could say that this was the moment where my life turned around, but it wasn't. It was a start, but it wasn't the end of my "BC" life (before Christ). The good news was that it was the moment I left my boyfriend, dropped out of college in Colorado, moved home, and quit drugs cold turkey.

God was filling me with the strength I needed to move forward, but I still did not actually know who God was, who I was, or who I wasn't. For the first month, I had severe withdrawals. When you come off of drugs, like the drugs I had been on, you should go to the hospital and go through supervised detox. There are serious health precautions and things that could have gone very wrong, but I did not want anyone to know how bad it actually was. My shame and fear held me back from receiving the help I needed.

For a month, I couldn't walk up a hill without getting faint. I had no appetite. I was either extremely hot or extremely cold. I was having constant anxiety and panic attacks whenever I was in public because my senses were overloaded with sounds and sights. I actually developed extremely bad vertigo, which inhibited me from taking elevators or going up too high. I am about five foot five, and I was about ninety pounds. I was so skinny that the doctor thought I was anorexic and offered me serious help.

I was too scared to tell her what was actually going on. I did not know how to communicate my feelings. I truly believed that no one would love me and that everyone would reject me.

Luckily for me, even though my family did not really know what was going on with me, they were extremely loving and supportive. My mom would bring me anything I needed, my dad would go on walks with me and sit with me on the couch, and my sister and brother extended love and support to me. God and my family were getting me through that hard time.

I began going to our family's church. I started singing to God and praying to God, but I still did not actually have a relationship with Jesus or understand the Bible. I did not know what following Jesus looked like, and I really was not ready to actually lay down my entire life. I only wanted to lay down the parts that I realized were not working. Even though I was not ready to fully surrender, I really wanted to do better. I wanted to have a better life. That led me to apply to small Christian colleges around Southern California. I believed that going to a school like that would keep me on track.

How many times in life do we think that moving somewhere or changing our group of friends will change what is going on internally? You see, although those external factors were important to change, I still was taking the main problem with me: me.

In a miracle, I got into Pepperdine University with an extremely low GPA. I was so excited to have a fresh start and to make a new name for myself. Although I had quit doing drugs, I did not have a firm foundation in Jesus yet. I quickly got sucked in by Satan into many other sinful habits. Again, I was misled by this idea that you can be a Christian but still do whatever you want, whenever you want. I did not want to obey what the Bible told me. I still viewed God and the Word of God as condemning concepts that would limit and control my free will. I did not understand the goodness of who God really is and the abundant life that He had in store for me.

I took the parts that I liked from Christianity, and I left the rest behind, claiming that it was not important—when all of the Bible is without error and all of God's Word is to be obeyed. For my whole life, I had believed in God, but I didn't believe in God. Confusing? Yes, I know. So of course I was confused too. That led me down a very cloudy path of confusion and chaos. I was seeking God, but I was looking for other people to tell me who He was. People were telling me that parts of the Bible were old and didn't matter—while also believing that the Bible is inspired by God. It was a total mess. To provide clarity, the Bible is inspired by God—and it is without error. Everything in the Bible is valid, and no part is to be left out.

Since I was not personally seeking Him, I was majorly confused. I was vulnerable and ready to take anything I could get. Satan likes this stage of life. He sees the vulnerability and comes in with distractions to try to throw us off course. When we are ready to believe in something, Satan comes with the perfect temptation, and it seems so real and so good.

Chapter 6

When I got to Pepperdine, I became friends with a group of individuals who claimed to be followers of Christ, but only some really were. Some are still my best friends today, and I love them dearly. I wish I was friends with some other people, but I dismissed them because they did not like to party and live a half Christian life like I did. By the way, that is not a thing; you are either all in or you are all out. The ones I wish I was friends with were all in, as it should be, but I was not. So I avoided the all-in people. Even after watching God move mountains like addictions and abuse out of my life, I still was not all in. It is hard to believe, but faith is hard—I would even argue it is impossible—when we do not know our Creator personally. We all knew of God, but we never made Him a priority in our lives.

I was close though, and Satan saw me as a threat. He came at me from a new angle to get me to fall behind once more. Since I was not fully planted on the truth, Satan fed me a lie. It is so important that we have a firm foundation rooted in Jesus. Satan used what I had struggled with, and suppressed, for my whole life. Within moments, he brought it all back out. I was looking for something to fill me, and I was so close to having it be Jesus, but it just did not happen that way.

Satan brought a girl into my life, and that ended up starting a whole new season of my life. Like in Proverbs 5, she was a beautiful smooth talker, and she had a magnetic pull to her that I cannot explain. You might be able to see where this is going, especially after reading the beginning of the book. We are diving headfirst into the area that I am most passionate about: the area that had the biggest hold on me before Jesus.

Since I was in a sorority in Colorado, I immediately was in the same one at Pepperdine. My husband and all of my friends now are still confused about how I was in a sorority, but that is beside the point. My life was very incongruent, but I was a chameleon. I had many different identities.

I met a group of girls in the sorority who were awesome, and I quickly became good friends with a few of them. For a Taco Tuesday, we all went over to my friend's apartment for tacos and margaritas. I haven't mentioned it yet, but I smoked cigarettes too. I went outside to have a cigarette with the girl who I was intrigued by. We sat on the stairs, smoking, and she told me how she had secretly been dating a girl from the sorority. I wondered, *If it is a secret, why is she trusting me? I am a complete stranger.*

After talking, she drove me back to my place and dropped me off. Nothing happened, but part of me did want something to. A week or so later, we decided to all go out one night to a club in Santa Monica. After a long and fun night, this girl and I were in the back of an Uber. She laid down on my lap and looked up at me. As we made eye contact, we began to share an intimate kiss. The butterflies going on in my stomach were surreal. It was new, I was nervous, and I was captivated. Little did I know that this kiss would set the next few years of my life on a new track.

There was something about the kiss, not the girl, that intrigued me. It was this feeling that I never once had gotten after kissing a boy. I just was in awe; sin had me captivated. I started to think for days and weeks about it. I wondered if I was what the world called a *lesbian*.

Time went by, and I was extremely confused about my life and what was going on. This girl happened to not be interested in me, so it was a wild ride of rejection on that front because I tried to connect with her. I wanted to continue to feel out my emotions, but she was not interested. She and the girl she had been secretly dating were in the middle of some drama.

Ironically, I ended up talking a lot with her ex-girlfriend at the time. They were both pretty much using me the whole time, but I ended up really developing feelings this time. We began doing the classic millennial way of getting to know one another. We snapchatted and texted all day, every day.

Before I knew it, we were meeting up for the first time at my house. I was living in Calabasas, sharing a house with five other girls from school. She came over to the house and met with me. We just sat on the couch and started to get to know each other. Everything was still so new to me—these new feelings and the new school—and I was just in a euphoric state of mind. It was exciting. I am someone who loves change, and I love a good rush of emotions. I have an addictive personality. She had already been dating the girl who was mentioned before, but I had never dated a girl. I was nervous, but she started to get closer and closer. As we began to kiss, I felt the same feeling that I felt in the back of the Uber. It was a high that I just wanted more of. It was something new, something I could cling to, something to fulfill me.

That euphoric feeling was something I had never experienced. It clung closer than drugs ever did. Sin has a way of clinging closely like that to us. It makes us feel like it is the answer we have been looking for our entire lives. I immediately began to live out a homosexual lifestyle. I mean, it just started to make sense. Everything around me, everything I had gone through, was all starting to make sense. The false sense of security, the false sense of satisfaction, and the false sense of fulfillment became my new drugs.

I actually began to really develop feelings. It was the first relationship I had ever been in, and I actually felt love. What I felt for her was real. We began dating, secretly, with only a few close friends knowing, for almost two years. We were in a closeted relationship, and nothing about that can be healthy.

As our relationship got deeper, I began to find myself sacrificing everything I had ever wanted or dreamed of for that girl and that lifestyle. I always wanted to be married to a man and have our own children, but somewhere along the line, I deemed myself unworthy of that dream and gave it all up. Remember that story about the drainage area and the ocean? This was that moment for me. I thought I had found the person I was going to marry. I told her that I would allow her to bear children, because I knew how much she wanted it, instead of me. We had plans to raise a family together, and even though I was excited, it was nothing I actually wanted. I was so willing to give up everything I knew I could have received to just be happy in that one moment. I didn't know that I was actually longing for eternal joy.

We can take a look at the story of Esau in the Bible and see how real this is. Esau was promised to be extremely powerful;

God had a big plan for him. However, Jacob, Esau's brother, was making food, and Esau was starving. Esau got super dramatic, and started exclaiming that he was so hungry he would die! So Jacob offered Esau the food in exchange for his birthright (the promises of God). Esau, out of a desire for instant gratification and fulfillment, took the food and forfeited his birthright.

I did that too. I knew, deep down inside of me, that I deserved more. I knew I had dreams, goals, and promises ahead of me. I really wanted to be a mother and a wife. I wanted to be pregnant and experience the joy it would bring. I wanted a husband who was trustworthy, loyal, kind, funny, and handsome. I was so blinded by love, instant satisfaction, and excitement that I was willing to give up my future. It was weird. I had dreams, yet I was fighting them. I do not know why I always did that. I always stopped myself. I always took myself out of the race. It is so heartbreaking what insecurity and fear can do to a vision.

Have you ever done this? Have you ever seen potential and promises and then thrown it all away for temporary, instant satisfaction? We need to change our perspective. We need to set our eyes on the long game and focus on the future. Living for the now has never done anyone a service, and I hate to break it to you, but you are not the exception. What we do now will create what our future looks like. Being carefree is not being free; it is being immature and reckless. God has so much in store for each and every one of us. He literally promises us everything that belongs to Him, which is the entire world and everything in it. He gives us power and authority over life. I wish I knew about that concept back then. God has so many promises for you, but with every promise comes a battle! That is why we must learn how to stand firm and know the truth.

What I felt was real. Although it was not actually freedom, it felt like it. That is why I will never downplay people for practicing homosexuality. I understand where they are coming from, and I want you to understand it as well. I have no doubt that people who do not know Jesus can feel love, peace, happiness, and freedom. However, I also have no doubt that they are not experiencing the true versions of those feelings. People who do know Jesus can feel true love, a peace that surpasses all understanding, an everlasting joy, and actual freedom. It was all I knew and what I believed in. How was I supposed to know that what I was feeling wasn't all that was out there for me? I thought it was as good as love was ever going to get. I began thinking, *If God is real, and God is love, wouldn't He want me to love this girl? Wouldn't He love that I am in love?* I lacked an understanding of the truth and of the Word of God.

I started claiming that commandments in the Bible allow homosexuality; in reality, the Bible is very clear about how the act of homosexuality is a sin. I wanted to justify how I felt, and so I did. I surrounded myself with people who believed the same thing as me, and I found a church community that encouraged me to pursue my own desires. We claimed that the Bible's number one commandment was to love others, and we used that as a basis for our own self-righteousness. Let me say this clearly: The Bible's first commandment is to love God.

> Jesus replied: "Love the Lord your God with all
> your heart and with all your soul and with all your

mind." This is the first and greatest commandment. And the second is like it: "Love your neighbor as yourself." (Matthew 22:37–39 NIV)

Loving God allows us to love others as He loves us. If we are loving ourselves and others before loving God, we are unfortunately and dangerously out of order. I was out of order. The closer to sin I got, the deeper into the homosexual lifestyle I went—and the further I went from God. Can you relate to that? We cannot have two masters. If God is not first, we are out of order. A lot of us blame God when it is us who are out of order.

Unfortunately, I blamed God all the time. Growing up, I had always believed I was supposed to be a boy. I hated being a girl. Truly, every fiber in my being wanted to be a boy. I felt robbed. Why didn't I get to be born the gender I wanted to be born? I constantly felt like boys had such a better life than girls. I resented God for creating me as a girl. I was not loving God, but I did not actually understand who He was, how much He loves us, and what that really means for us. The good news is that it really is good news! Instead of accepting that I was made perfect in His sight, as a daughter of His, I fought Him and complained. I acted like He did not know what He was doing.

Since I always wanted to be a boy, I took on the more masculine role of the relationship. It started to feel like I could actually be myself. I could wear edgy clothes, not worry about makeup and hair, and just embrace what I perceived to be my true identity. This girl, and every girl for that matter, I dated, were all extremely feminine, well-dressed, makeup done, and drop-dead gorgeous girls. They were girly, gossipy, and dramatic. They were everything that I wasn't. I mention things like "drop-dead gorgeous" because I find it interesting that I began dating the girls who I was always jealous of. Everything that I was insecure about, they were confident about. I didn't know this at the time, but what I actually loved most about them was this idea that they completed me. I was seeking femininity more than I was seeking love. Everything that I was lacking, they brought into my life. The femininity I could not achieve, they achieved for me. I felt like I no longer had to compete with girly girls because I was now dating them. It was an attempt on my part, a way to try to fill up the emptiness inside of myself. The areas in me where I thought a boy would never love because I was deficient were the areas that these girls appreciated and admired.

Let's look into this a little closer. The way that God designed marriage was for two people who are different to come together as one, thus completing one another, right? I did not even realize that we all have that innate desire that God created us with and designed us to have; it makes sense now why I sought out a girl who would complete me. What I see now is it wasn't anything more than that. Were there real feelings involved? Yes. Was I on a search for something much deeper than just a relationship? Yes. I was operating out of the innate way that God has designed every human being: a desire to be complete, to be fulfilled, to be loved, to be respected for who we are. I was so close, yet so far. Right desires, wrong places. It seems like a common idea where the ways of this world are so close, mimicking the ways of the Lord, but they fall short of ultimate fulfillment and freedom.

Now, going back to my relationship with this girl. As I said, it was real. I am not denying any of my feelings, and I really want to get that point across. I also am not glamorizing or promoting sinful behaviors; we just have to realize there is a reason why sin is so enticing. That is why we all fall to it.

My intentions are to bring awareness that sin is enticing, and it is hard for anyone to shake off any sin that clings so close to them that it becomes their identity. We are often easier on ourselves about this subject than we are with other people who are fighting a hard battle. I see differently now, but it was real to me at the time.

As a church, we need to comprehend that; a lot of that is the reason why I am writing this book. We need compassion and empathy. I want everyone to understand what it is like on the other side of the LGBTQ world. Somewhere along the line, we took homosexual behaviors so far away from all other sin, but it wasn't shocking to Jesus, and it shouldn't be shocking to us. There is a need to normalize it and understand it for what it is: a sin. It is part of a broken world that God is redeeming and restoring, and He will redeem and restore in full one day soon.

Unfortunately, this relationship took a bad turn for me. There was a lot that happened during this time. I still was experimenting with boys and girls. I was calling myself bisexual some days and homosexual other days. I even dated a guy for a bit of time. He was a super great guy, but at the end of the day, we were just messing around, as always. However, this girl had my heart.

Since I had dropped out for a semester in college, I was a semester behind. All of my friends were graduating, and I was hanging around with the guy. After graduation, my ex-girlfriend and I decided to start things up again. At the beginning of summer, I went on vacation, and she returned home to where her family lived. We had been on and off for all of our relationship, but something weird happened. I got ghosted. Classic millennials, I know. If you do not know what that means, basically she stopped texting and calling me—and just disappeared from life. After more than a year together, going through the most intimate transformational time of our lives, she just disappeared.

She was someone I believed I was going to spend the rest of my life with, and you can understand how this left me in the lowest place I had ever been in. I constantly threw myself at her, trying to get her to reach back out to me. It was embarrassing, but I was broken. My identity was based in that relationship. I faced the hard truth of when we put our hope in another person. I had viewed her like she was my god, and quite frankly, I think she knew that. She loved the attention. I was vulnerable and needed a god, and I made her into it. When she left me, I felt abandoned by God. Interesting, right? I put my hope in a person, in an identity, and when that false god was exposed, it somehow made me feel hurt by the real God. It breaks my heart that we are so quick to blame God for our mistakes and our pain when God did not cause it.

I was working at a restaurant in Malibu, finishing my last semester in college, and living in an oceanfront studio apartment. My life looked solid on the outside, but my heart was broken. Every day when I was at work, I had this dream, a fairy tale, that she would come walking in through the door. I was waiting and hoping for something, but I was getting nothing. At one point, I was sitting in the bathtub and got the closest I had ever gotten to committing suicide. I called a close friend, and after being talked out of it, I white-knuckled through a lot of pain. It was a lot like the first time it happened. Unfortunately, this time, I did not turn to God.

I went right back into a party lifestyle and officially took my label from bisexual to homosexual. I was hanging out and dating girls for a while. I met a girl on an online dating app for women seeking out women. Since homosexuality is often closeted, it is a big thing to find each other through an app. This was before it was extremely common for heterosexuals too. I found a pretty girl and went for it since everything in my life was always based on lust and physical attraction. She came over one night, and we just hit it off. We took the relationship to another level really fast, right away.

It was my way of coping with the past relationship. I took all of the rejection and the pain that I felt, and I invested everything into this new relationship. I guess you can say that she was what we call a rebound. This rebound turned into a big deal though because that was the relationship where she really encouraged me to tell my friends and family about what was going on. I became friends with her friends, and they are some of the most influential LGBTQ activists in Los Angeles and in the country. I was a closeted chameleon surrounded by people whose jobs it was to promote their homosexual lifestyle. She and all of our friends were very forward and loved to post things on social media. That was all new for me, and I was not sure if I was ready for that. However, I needed to fit in. That was my new West Hollywood circle, and something had to give. It was me; I gave in.

I started dating her, and she continued to tell me that she really felt like I needed to tell people and needed to express myself. She wholeheartedly believed that I was a homosexual, and I took what she said to heart and went forward with it.

On Thanksgiving, after we had been dating for a while, I realized I just wanted to be open when I was around my family. I just wanted to be honest, and I wanted them to know what was going on. I wanted to be free. I didn't want to hide anymore. I was definitely being pressured, and my insides were all shook up constantly, but I just had to go for it.

This is where I want to make a connection for you. For decades, human beings have enslaved the LGBTQ community. As I mentioned, we have abused them, locked them up, tortured them, pressured them, judged them, and shunned them. By the way, that is not love. Injustice and hate are never okay. Anywhere that there is captivity, there is freedom on the other side. Perhaps by treating one another so poorly, we have actually created a version of freedom, but that is not what God intended freedom to be. When God calls us into true freedom with Him, we expose ourselves and follow Him. There is a supernatural realm that gives us peace, love, and joy that we cannot explain without the Holy Spirit. On earth, we have created a tangible freedom that does not need supernatural help because we have caused injustice and enslavement. Many people seek out freedom.

God calls us to set captives free. This looks like many things, and it can be done in many ways, but the biggest is to stop hating, start loving, and lead people into the presence of the Holy Spirit.

The LGBTQ community sought freedom from the oppression of people, but true freedom is accepting Jesus's relief of our oppression of sin. I just wanted to walk around holding hands with my girlfriend. I just wanted to be able to express my emotions without people judging me or rejecting me. I just wanted to be able to wear whatever clothes I wanted to wear without everyone staring at me. You get the idea. I felt like I was literally trapped in a closet, and coming out of that closet feels like the freest you might ever be. However, I am proposing and claiming that there is a supernatural freedom that far exceeds this freedom. That is where we no longer are slaves to sin. We are free—thanks to Jesus!

That year, I left Thanksgiving early. On my way home to Malibu, I went home to my parents' house and wrote a letter to my sister telling her about my sexuality and lifestyle. I told her that I was dating a girl. I have no reason why I chose my sister to be the one who I wanted to know first. It was like God knew my sister was who I needed to hear what was going on because He knew that she was who He was going to use to bring me into a relationship with Him. My sister was always who God sent me to, in the good and the bad, but I never realized it.

As photos came out and my family and friends found out, word eventually got out. Everyone started asking me questions and telling me it wasn't me and that I was not serious. I just started getting really overwhelmed. Everyone talks about the coming-out process where there are people who support you and there are people who judge you. As far as I knew, that was me. I did not want to hear from anyone who was telling me that what I was feeling was not okay. I started pushing everyone away and clinging to the people in my life who encouraged my lifestyle. After all, the world's definition of freedom is to do whatever you want and not let anyone hold you back from doing it. I closed my ears off to everyone—unless they supported me. I had no room for opposition or even just real talk.

Through this all, I am so grateful for my family. If you are a parent or a family member who has a close one dealing with the sin of homosexuality, please love them. Please hear me out. Sexual sin is equal with all other sin. It does not make anyone worse than anyone else. We need to take all sin seriously, and we also need to treat all sin the same. We cannot categorize sin into man-made levels. We are all creations of God, and we are all humans. Please never shun anyone or turn your back on them because they are falling into sin.

I watched my family handle it the best they could. While no one is perfect, and it was definitely hard for them to handle it appropriately because it was so unexpected, they did the best they could. I will forever admire them for that. It was wonderful because they followed the lead of God. They told me they loved me and would never leave me because I was family, but they told me if I chose to live a life without God, then I had to own it. They would not support it. That was the truth, but I did not want to hear it. More than that, I am sure it was even harder for them to say it. I wanted to hear that my decisions were the right decisions. I wanted them to agree with my truth and not God's truth. Unfortunately, at the time, I did not receive what they were saying to me. I took it as abandonment. I ran away, choosing to leave my family behind, and followed what I believed to be my truth.

That was the hardest season of my life. I felt free, but I felt so much pain. The two should not go hand in hand. There was a lot going on. The girl I was dating saw what I was going through, and she decided we should break up. My family was shocked and still did not agree with my views and my decisions.

My job was ending because the restaurant that I was co-managing was being bought out by a new owner. I had just graduated college and had zero direction. Of course, I did what I did best. I went to West Hollywood to party with some friends. I felt free, but I felt so much pain. That is not freedom.

Although it was the hardest season of my life, I know now that it was the hardest season of my parents' life as well. They were so confused and had no idea what the right thing to do was. However, God showed them. Take a look at the story of Moses's birth:

> Now a man of the tribe of Levi married a Levite woman, and she became pregnant and gave birth to a son (Moses). When she saw that he was a fine child, she hid him for three months. But when she could hide him no longer, she got a papyrus basket for him and coated it with tar and pitch. Then she placed the child in it and put it among the reeds along the bank of the Nile. His sister stood at a distance to see what would happen to him. (Exodus 2:1–4 NIV)

This baby being talked about is Moses. Pharaoh had ordered all male babies born to be taken and sent down the Nile. Moses's mom tried her best to take care of him and hide him as long as she could. When she realized she could not protect him any longer, she let him go. She trusted God.

Moses ended up in the hands of God and lived an abundant and amazing life. Moses's mom realized she could not control her son's outcome on her own, but she had enough faith to let

Chapter 7

I feel like I have gone through enough of the messy part of my message! Although this book may seem kind of dark, I really wanted to give you an idea of who I was and who I am now—as an autobiography should do. However, for me, the best part of a story is the happy ending! If I didn't talk about all of the bad, then you would not be able to see how good God really is! So now that you understand the brokenness of my life—and I have let you in on a lot of things about me that no one ever really knew—it is time to take you into the best part of my life. This is the part where I find the freedom that my free-spirited heart always longed for.

I found myself out of the relationship I had been in, and I had few real friends and no family support. I had just graduated, but I had no direction. I had really hit my bottom. We used to go out every night in West Hollywood, and one night, after hanging out behind a dumpster with some homeless friends, behind a bank, I realized that I didn't have the life I wanted. I looked in the mirror the next morning and realized that I could not even recognize myself. I started to see clearly, but I was still confused.

I hit my knees and cried out to the God who had helped me before. I went back to my apartment in Malibu, and I slept it all off. I woke up the next day and texted my sister that I needed God—and that I needed help. My family wept with joy and welcomed me home with open arms. I love them so much.

That week, before actually moving home, my sister invited me to church in Los Angeles. I walked around this modern church, and said, "There is no way that all of these good-looking young people are Christians." When I saw all the famous people there, I was in complete shock. I always thought Christians were all boring old people who lived sad lives. Sorry, but unfortunately, that is what our image looks like to the non-Christian world. My mind was blown.

After a sermon on surrender, the pastor got up and said, "I feel like there is someone here today who God has moved mountains in your life before, and He wants you to know that He can do it again." They then played "Do It Again" by Elevation Worship. I fell into my sister's arms and started crying for the second time. I raised my hand during the altar call, and I cried and sang. This time, I could feel the Holy Spirit. Something inside of me felt different, and I just felt okay. As I cried and looked around at thousands of people worshiping Jesus, I felt surrounded by peace and love. Mountains were being moved again, but this time, it was different. This time, I was ready to give my entire life to Christ, including my sexuality.

I was only about twenty-one at the time. I am so grateful that God pulled me out at such a young age. That's why my passion is to help stir up a voice and stir up a thought so that people can receive the goodness of God at a young age. They don't have to hit rock bottom in order to find Jesus at a later age. I believe we can reach children at a young age. They can know who God is. They can know who made them, and they can know who that means they are not. I believe that children can give their lives to Christ, out of pure joy and love, and God can protect them and keep them in His goodness for the rest of their lives. I want children to experience what I never got to experience. I want children to avoid experiencing everything that I did experience.

Shortly after that powerful encounter, I moved back to my family's house and began going to church again. This time, it was genuine. I began going every Sunday, I read my Bible every day, I joined a women's small group, and I started serving. The women's small group changed my life. In the group, I never felt more alive. Being surrounded by Christians who did not act like they were perfect was so refreshing to me. I finally felt like I fit in somewhere.

I surrounded myself with Jesus and with people who could point me to Him. There were many angels who came into my life at that time. They listened to me, they never judged me, and they prayed for healing over me. The first time I walked into the group, I sat by myself in the back corner. I was dressed in pajamas, wondering why I was at church on a Friday night. Then, out of the corner of my eye, I saw an older lady coming toward me. She sat down and started talking to me. She was my angel. She got me into their women's small group on Monday nights, and I started meeting women going through battles like I was.

These women listened to me, talked with me, cared for me, and encouraged me. They helped me love myself until I could receive God's love. Relationships with the same sex are very important for people coming out of the LGBTQ lifestyle. It's something that can seriously transform and change lives. It did for me. It was so crucial for me to understand that we can have relationships with the same sex that are not sexually based and that God can do so much transformation and redemption through those kinds of relationships. As a church body, we need to really be there for one another and understand that God wants to use us in life-transforming ways. I was so scared—and sometimes I still am—that women in the church will think I am different than them and not want to be friends. Let us understand this insecurity and be available to God and to others. Be present and let the Holy Spirit help you be willing to step out of your comfort zone and embrace what God has called us all here to embrace.

Once I received God's love and really learned who He is, my whole life changed dramatically. For the first time, I was building relationships with women on a nonsexual basis. I had other female friends before, but this time, it was different. I felt known and loved by women on a deep spiritual basis. It was fulfilling a deep desire within my heart to feel loved. I also felt like they were not judging me or thinking that I liked them as more than a friend, but they just saw me as an equal and as a friend.

Even though it was the best year of my life, it was also the most challenging. Following God is not easy, but it is always worth it. The moment I started following God, all of my exes started reaching out to me again. It was the craziest thing. It was so hard to say no, especially to the girl who I really did love, but I knew God had bigger and better things for me. There was a lot of fighting in that area.

A lot of times, we see the ocean ahead, but we get caught up in the sewage. This was that decision point for me. Would I turn back to what I feel like I wanted in the moment or hold out and go for what God was putting in front of me? I chose to keep going forward, thankfully, but it was hard. There was also a lot of doubt and a lot of questioning God. There was a lot of judgment from my non believing friends. There was a lot of isolation. I really was starting my life over from the ground up. It was a brand-new way of life. Leaving your old life and following Jesus is a giant step, and it is a hard step. I lost all my friends, I stopped being intimate with people, I stopped drinking, I stopped smoking, and I changed my career and my direction. You name it, I was in it. God did not make me do any of things; I *chose* to do them. I was filled with the Holy Spirit, and I was listening to Him every step of the way—joyfully! Still, it was rough. It was all so new to me.

What makes it rougher is how Satan puts a magnetic pull on sin. Something draws you in spiritually, without you noticing it and without you having the power to turn it away. I felt like sin was being thrown at me left and right. It felt like it was more tempting than ever before.

It was so awesome though! That was the first time I saw that negative magnetic pull starting to go away. God had renewed my mind. I did not see the world like I used to; my appetites for life were beginning to change completely. A real transfiguration process had begun.

I saw God helping me change my life. The neuropathways that always led me to drugs or sex or homosexuality were now blocked, and I was creating new ones. It was like I suddenly loved worship music, hated cuss words, hated injustice, and made it my mission to help others avoid what I had gone through.

I saw God blessing me with His provision, favor, and security. My life was full of blessings that I did not deserve. I did not bring anything into this world. I did not even deserve to be born, yet here I am. And even after years of fighting God and living in darkness, Jesus still chose me, He still died for me, and He still called me out. Jesus chased me down when He did not have to. Oh, the love of Jesus. He doesn't need me, but He has chosen me to help build His kingdom—and the same goes for you! God's favor, provision, and security are upon you. An abundant life, which you can't earn and don't deserve, is already with you! God is so good. He is so kind. If He can do it for me, He will do it for you!

I saw God creating a passion in me to get people to understand what true freedom looks like. When you are a new believer, it feels like God is lighting a fire under your butt. You can't sit down. You are just running around and screaming about the love of God! I began to understand what it means for God to take beauty from ashes. He began using the dirtiness of my life to change other people's lives. I wanted everyone around me to experience what I was experiencing.

Even though I was on fire for Christ, and I still am, it took a while to fully pray through the trials and change my life. I had to build new friendships and start over. I would be lying and doing a disservice to you if I told you that there were not any battles along the way. In fact, Satan was coming against me more than ever before, but I had God by my side. If there is spiritual opposition when you are walking with Christ, it means you are on the right path!

I did not know how to have fun without partying, and I did not know how to have a healthy view of friendships and intimacy. I never had a "normal" young adult life. It was challenging, but I felt overwhelming confidence, peace, joy, and freedom for the first time. That was the moment when I realized what true freedom was. It was building a relationship with the God who created me, communicating with him, connecting on a deep level, and accepting His will for my life and not my own. It was not tangible, and it was not circumstantial; it was internal, and it was supernatural.

Giving up sex and relationships for a while was by far the hardest thing I had ever had to do. I had never even gone on a real date before; all my relationships were based on sex. I had to seek God constantly to help me see myself as He sees me. Who was I? I couldn't answer this question on my own, but as I sought after God, He began showing me.

I made sticky notes with the words that God spoke over me, and put them on my mirror. "You are beautiful," "You are loved," and "You have a purpose." The biggest one for me was something that God specifically told me to write out and tell myself all day, every day: "Surrender to me, and I will show you true freedom. I will give you everything your heart desires, and my grace will be enough for you." Man, is that true—or what! I meditated day in and day out on God's words and His promises over my life.

I woke up every day, hit my knees, and prayed to God that He would remove everything that was bad inside of me. I prayed that He would remove all of the dirt, all of the negativity, and all of the fear, and then come into my life and fill me with His Word and His heart. I was in so much pain; homosexuality was something that I could not bear on my own. I could not do it on my own. I felt God picking it up for me. That was where my relationship with God took off; God carried me through it all, and I felt how much He loved me. I learned to trust Him and rely on Him. We need God to do the impossible because it shows us how badly we really need Him. I no longer had a need for anything else in the world; I was purely satisfied in Him. That is freedom. I was free for the first time in my life. I no longer just desired freedom; I *was* free. I was really free.

After about a year of focusing on my relationship with Jesus and letting him cleanse me from the inside out, I started going to graduate school for a master's in teaching. I had always loved children, and I had always known that I wanted to be in a career based around helping them grow. After three days of classes, God clearly told me that teaching was not my calling. I did not agree with many of the things that are being taught today, and I knew that teaching those things would be a direct contradiction to my life. God knew that if I had become a teacher in the public school system, I would have eventually been required by law to teach children, as early as kindergarten, about every different gender affiliation and sexual orientation. This book and my thoughts would have appeared inconsistent and unsure, and I now better understand that "no."

I dropped out and prayed for direction. He told me to go to the church where I had been serving and ask to get into children's ministry there. I started going to seminary, and I started working in children's ministry as paid staff. It was amazing, and I loved working at the church that had blessed me so much. I was only working part-time, but I knew distinctly that God was calling me into full-time ministry. I thought that only highly qualified Christians who had been in the church for thirty years got to lead in ministry, but God showed me otherwise. His favor was upon me, and He equipped me in ways that I cannot even explain. My heart was full. I had found my calling, but I had no idea where I was going or how to get there.

After a little while, I began to feel God stirring my heart to pray about a husband. This scared me endlessly because I did not think I was ready. I had tried to date some guys in the church, but nothing was working out. I was losing hope in the whole marriage thing. I told God I would honor Him all of my days even if He called me to singleness. If I was called to singleness, I considered running an orphanage and taking in as many children as I could. Maybe one day I still will.

I started laughing and questioning Him, but He spoke so clearly to me. He said, "Chloe, my heart was never for you to just give everything up for me because I want to control you and take things away from you; my heart is for you to give everything up for me so that I can give you what you truly desire and deserve."

I saw God in a different light in that moment. I felt the lovingness of the Father. I felt how much He really cared for me and how much He cares for all of His children. I also understood the misguidance of "conversion therapy" and why most of what it has done is cause confusion. I understood why old-school Christian tactics never worked. God is so loving, and so generous; He is so good. He wanted me to seek Him first. He wanted me to not want anything more than to just be in His presence. He met me where I was, held my hand through everything, and then brought me into the light. He carried what I could not. He just wanted my heart. It is crazy how we hold on to things so tightly, but as soon as we trust God—not just with words, but truly trust God in the innermost part of our soul—He blows our minds.

Chapter 8

After a lot of time removing darkness, renewing my mind, and transforming my heart, God removed what was broken and began redeeming things left and right. God was urging me to believe and pray for a husband. In November, I was reading a book about praying powerful prayers. I began to really ask God to provide me with romantic love. I wanted to be married, and I believed that God would honor that because I am a child of God! During one of those fierce prayers, God spoke to me the number seventeen. I had no idea what it meant, and the Lord had never spoken to me like that before. The voice was so loud, and the number was so clear. I wrote it in my journal, but for two months, I could not figure out what it meant.

By January, I had kind of moved on. I figured that God would show me what it meant at some point, but I did not know how. One Sunday evening, I was working at church. After our six o'clock service, I decided to go to the young adult event—even though they were super boring. Something was just nudging me to stop by that night. I saw a high school girl I was mentoring and hanging out with at the time, and her friend urged me to meet her brother. I was not interested. I had not really been attracted to males, I did not look good, and I had worked all day. It was the last thing I wanted to do, but I said okay.

I sat down next to my now husband, Trent, and he asked me two questions. He asked, "Are you tough?"

You can't even guess what I did. It was super feminine. Just kidding. I flexed my bicep.

He felt my muscle, and we laughed.

He asked, "Do you love Jesus?"

I replied, "More than anything."

The night went on, and after the event, he invited me to go rock climbing. It was nine o'clock on a Sunday; I was confused and said no. After a couple repeat questions, he got me to agree to going with him. I went home to change.

About a week before, I had been watching a country music show with my mom. Tim McGraw and Faith Hill sang "The Rest of Our Life." I looked at my mom and said, "That is the song that I will get married to." She laughed and said that I was no Faith Hill since she was a "good girl."

When Trent picked me up, "The Rest of Our Life" was playing on the radio.

I asked, "Do you know this song?"

He said, "No. I just turned on the radio, and it was on."

I was a bit shocked, but we carried on. We showed up to the rock-climbing gym, and it was like we were on an episode of *The Bachelor*. The gym was closed and empty, but they let us in. We had the best time together, even though I am scared of heights, and then we went and got ice cream.

Trent drove me to a spot overlooking the beach cities, and I was in awe. It was the same spot where I used to park my car and do drugs during high school. It had redemption written all over it. We sat on the hood of his jeep and talked for hours. By the end of the night, we knew everything about each other. There was no judgment, no hate; it was intentional and loving.

I had never been on a date that wasn't based on excitement or lust. When I got home, I was a bit confused and in awe. I started journaling. As I wrote the date on the top of the page, I noticed that it was January 7 (1/7). I immediately knew Trent was the man God was giving to me to take care of me for the rest of my life. It was a bit overwhelming, but it was not surprising. In the beginning of my walk with Jesus, He loved blowing my mind, miracle after miracle, and proving who He was to me. He still does it daily, but it was so special at that time.

I was done being a crazy girl, so I couldn't tell him that. After one date, I couldn't say we were going to get married. However, we dated literally every day after that, and little did I know that Trent was receiving prophetic dreams about me and marriage. He had a dream one night, that he was holding my hand. We were walking. He asked where we were going, and I replied, "You will find out on February 2."

I never knew about his dream, but on February 2, we were driving down the coast, after celebrating his birthday in Pismo Beach, and I pulled off randomly because I felt like exploring. We started walking through lush trees and butterflies, and when I grabbed his hand, his jaw dropped. He grabbed me and looked at me, and in that moment, he knew that was it. He looked at me like I have never been looked at before. I never knew eyes could say so much, but they did in that moment. We both knew we were going to marry one another, and nothing but pure peace and joy came over us. It was a love that we did not ask for or earn; it was a love that God called us to.

After two intentional and beautiful months, we were engaged. We got married that summer on July 21, 2018. All of my friends were definitely thinking, *There goes crazy Chloe.* My family was definitely nervous that it was moving so fast, but I knew it was God. Our confidence in our relationship won everyone over. I think my family was just elated that I had found a Christian male to spend the rest of my life with. Once the shock went away, it was all joy. Luckily for me, my husband is also the best human ever. He has a heart like Jesus's heart, and a heart after Jesus's, so everyone loves him—and they love him more each day.

The past two years have been the most challenging and most rewarding years of my life. Through every trial and every struggle, I have not had the desire to do drugs. I have never doubted my love for my husband. He truly is my greatest miracle. My greatest joy is getting to do life with him and watching God shape us into godly people more and more each day. He is really good-looking too. He is a paramedic—and will soon be a firefighter—and he is extremely smart. I could write a whole book about the amazing man that he is, but for now I will just keep thanking God every day for His greatest gift to me. It's heartbreaking that I deemed myself unworthy of such a man and such a love for so long, but it is nothing short of spectacular that God provides more for us than we could ever wish for or imagine. Life with my husband is always loving, always fun, and always fulfilling. He makes me complete.

When all of this was going on, my family was just in awe of how much fruit was suddenly being produced in my life. My family and I have a wonderful relationship now. We all saw God work a miracle in my life, and it has forever changed the dynamic of my family. God did so much more than just save me and give me a story. He uses my story as His story. I am constantly pointing people to Him and explaining how He is a God of the impossible.

People at church who see my husband and I have no idea about the life I lived before. They always say things to us about how our marriage is inspiring because we are so filled with joy and love. They look up to us. They say they want a marriage like ours. Isn't that amazing? God can use the most broken people in the most beautiful ways. He did not just give me a marriage; He gave me a marriage that would heal, inspire, and serve others. My husband and I laugh all the time because of how people view us now and how they would have viewed us in the past! Never give up on people. You never know. You just never know. God was, is, and will always be a miracle worker, no matter who the person is or what the circumstance is.

Many miracles were happening during that time. I had the privilege of working and training under some of the most amazing pastors at two different churches in California. My husband and I have found a home now. There is nothing better than a church that is not just a church, but it is home.

We are currently children's pastors at Oceans Church, a new church in Orange County, California, that is thriving under amazing pastoral leadership. I am twenty-five, and Trent is twenty-four. We are children of God, husband and wife, children's pastors, and homeowners. I am an author, and Trent is a paramedic. We are also starting a family; we have our first baby, a baby boy, due in October 2020! Life is so good. Each year brings more joy and more blessings. God truly designs marriage to be two people who bring out the best in one another and share in passion and vision. Our hearts are united. Our passion is to help everyone, especially children, know who God is, know who they are in Him, and find freedom. We look to raise up a generation of world changers who will be revivalists! We are so blessed. There is something about just loving God that allows so many blessings to come out. We are flourishing, and we have not done one thing to deserve it.

Another miracle is that my sister actually introduced my husband and me to Oceans Church. This is a miracle because my sister and I are in ministry together, and our relationship is healthier than ever. She was my maid of honor at my wedding, and I was honored to be hers as well. My sister and I were pretty much enemies our entire life before Christ. What used to be a broken relationship, with no way of being salvaged, is now mended and whole, thanks to Jesus. We were so different, and we still are, but there is something about coming together under Jesus's name that makes your differences insignificant. It is perfect unity and freedom. My story with my sister is a testament to the fact that even though we're all different in this world today, we are all the same. We were brought here for one purpose, and it is only made known when we understand who God is and help other people do the same.

Chapter 9

I am still in shock every day that I get to live this pure and amazing life. My life is not amazing because of force; my life is amazing now because the gentle Spirit of God is overwhelmingly loving and generous.

For decades, Christians have been trying to force conversion therapy onto the LGBTQ community. It is happening much less nowadays, but it still exists. While God calls us to change, no doubt about it, Christians judging and forcing their beliefs on others is not God's heart. God does not force anyone into change. God does not make us do anything. We should not be making or forcing anyone to do anything they do not want to do. That is not love. God was showing me that His goal was not to convert me from gay to straight—but from a sinner to a saint. He wanted to make me holy. All I wanted was to become more like Him. That is where the magic happened. The magic happened when my willingness and love for Jesus met His sovereignty.

We need to keep this in mind. I hope that anyone who is a part of the LGBTQ community will understand that the heart of Jesus is pure love. God is love. God sees everyone as so much more than their sin. His desire for us all is for us to find true freedom in Him. God accepts you just as you are, and He loves you just as you are. He invites you into a life with Him—no matter what you are doing or what your identity is. Like I said before, the conversion that God desires is to bring you from a sinner to a saint.

Our job as saints is to love one another. When we truly understand God's love, it gives us a picture of what love for one another looks like. We should not be labeling each other and ourselves by our sin; we should be asking the Holy Spirit to show us how He sees us. He gives us the strength and the kindness to love people who we do not see eye to eye with. We might not understand everyone, but the Holy Spirit will gladly equip us to do so. Our goal is to invite people into the presence of God and let God do the rest. God calls us to love and honor everyone, bringing unity and not division because of sin.

Let's show people who God really is. It is not too late. My heart longs to see Christians love and accept those who are gender ambiguous, gay, straight, male, female, black, white, homeless, or rich. We need to stop fearing others and we need to speak up in a world that needs our voice! My heart longs for Christians who are teaching that you can love Christ, be a saint, and live a homosexual lifestyle to rethink what they are preaching. I am so tired of hearing that the two go hand in hand because God is love and God wants us to love one another. Taking verses out of context to fit the world does nothing but confuse and mislead people! It confused and misled me. I am here now to make sure that no one else is misled; I want everyone to embrace the abundant and eternal life that Christ has for them.

When I was in the midst of a lot of confusion, so many pastors and churches were taking the commandment to love God and love others to justify homosexual behavior! There is no way to justify sinning against God. It breaks my heart when people who are hungry for the truth are fed lies. The truth should set people free and not enslave them. If Jesus was persecuted for telling the truth—and He was without sin and without fault—who are we to think that we need to change the Bible to avoid any persecution? The goal of the church is not to be loved by everyone; the goal of the church is to love everyone and free every captive.

When I was living a homosexual lifestyle and claiming that I was a Christian, so many people told me that I could be whoever I wanted to be—and God would still love me. And you know what? They were right—to an extent. What they were saying was true. God loves us all the time, no matter what. That is a fact. God never stops loving us, and He never leaves us—no matter who you are or what you have done. However, that was not the point they were trying to make. Pastors and peers who were saying these things to me were leading me to believe that Jesus approves of sin. Jesus does not approve of sin. In fact, He died so that we would not have to bear the punishment of our sin. Why would He die for our sin, if sin is good? The Bible doesn't say He died for a few, selective sins, it says He died for them all. Just a thought.

Jesus died for us while we were still sinners, and He loves us no matter what sin we struggle with. However, if we make our sin our master, and not Jesus, then we are missing something big. My concept of freedom became skewed because I thought, *I am free if I am a Christian, but I'm also free if I'm living my own life! So I can do both.* I think that's where we are wrong. You cannot have the world *and* God. You are either all in or all out. When you accept Jesus Christ as your Lord and Savior, you are literally accepting

Him as your Master. Therefore, you cannot live opposed to what your Master asks of you. Jesus makes it clear in the Bible that we cannot have two masters. This is instrumental in understanding how to build a firm faith foundation.

The way to building a firm faith is really just getting the basics down! When God created the world, he had a beautiful image in His mind. It was a beautiful world with an amazing sky, luscious green grass, flower beds, oceans, vegetation, animals, and birds. Everything was great! Everything was beautiful, but something was missing. That was why He created humankind.

God created a man named Adam, and when He noticed that Adam was alone, God created Eve, a woman, to pair with him. This was the first instance of male and female partnership. We were designed and created to be male and female, and we were made in the image of God. As males and females, we are made in the image of God. What makes us want to take that out of context? Why do humans want to remove the desire to be made in the image of God? Why are we running away from God? And why are so many people running away from God when they don't even know Him?

The answer is easy. People don't know we are in spiritual warfare. Churches are downplaying the spiritual realm. Where God is, Satan is also! Thanks to God, Satan has already lost. God has already won the war. That is good news! We serve a victorious God. He is the champion of the universe! However, there is also a scary part: people who are not walking with Jesus are actually walking with Satan. The worst part is that they do not even know it! We deny it and act as though it is nonexistent. It is time to be aware of what's going on.

Satan is very intentional in telling people that they do not have an identity. He has created the ultimate lie. As God said, the only sin that is against our own body is sexual sin. Satan has taken the sin that is against our own bodies—and distorted and disguised it. He is feeding everyone a lie. That lie is breaking up religions, breaking up families, breaking up our communities, and breaking up our politics. It's completely dividing the entire world right now!

Satan is lying and trying to convince people that it is actually creating unity, but you cannot create unity by applying the relative truth of every individual to this world. There are billions of people in this world, and we are the same. We are all creations of God. We are all human beings. We're all at the same level. We all have the same Creator, but we all have different minds and personalities. We cannot base our world off of the truth of many people; we can only base our world off of the truth of God. It is time to take the enemy's lies, expose them in the light, and allow God to move mightily. Let's reverse this global identity crisis that is going on.

Satan actually uses fragments of truth to confuse people. He takes a part of truth and twists it into a lie. That is why his lies are so easy to believe. That is why Eve was so quick to sin in the Garden of Eden. That is why we need to understand, as a generation today, that we cannot pick and choose the parts of the Bible that we want and leave the rest behind. We desperately need the Holy Spirit to help us navigate the Bible.

There is always a need for us to understand the fear of the Lord. The Bible states that the beginning of wisdom is the acceptance of the fear of the Lord into our lives. This does not mean being scared of God; it means that we honor Him, obey Him, and respect Him so much that we never want to hurt Him. Since I never honored God or feared Him, I did not mind when I did things that I knew broke His heart. However, I now draw so close to God—and fall so madly in love with Him—each day I wake up alive, and the desire for sin almost disappears. It feels like I understand the Bible from a much different angle now.

Just reading words out of a book and going to church won't do anything without the help of the Holy Spirit. God loves us, chooses us, and anoints us. We are here for Jesus and not for ourselves! Our lives are to be sacrificed out of love for Jesus and not out of obligation. It is not a negative thing; it's a life-giving thing. Laying down our lives and taking up the cross of Jesus is something we should do because we fully understand what Jesus has done for us. We're serving the God who created us and birthed us into existence! He owes us nothing; we owe Him everything. He deserves to have our utmost attention and all of our bodies, souls, and minds.

This message needs to be proclaimed to everyone in this world, and we cannot leave anyone out. We cannot let an entire group of people go unnoticed. We cannot back down from a spiritual war. As a church, we need to fight! We need to stand up, and we need to save this lost generation. We cannot back down because laws are being passed—and movements against God are occurring. We need to get up and start a new movement together. One that's going to change the world for God's glory!

Chapter 10

How do we change the world? We start by forming a personal relationship with Jesus. Only healed people can heal people. We all must take a look at our own lives and make sure that we are right with God before leading other people into His presence. We need to appropriately understand what is going on at a different level. We need the Holy Spirit to show us how to relate to people we do not relate to. We need to stand up for what is right.

We cannot fear the things of this world. Do you know what I fear most? I fear that I will just sit with my story and never share it because I am too scared of what people might think about me. If I were to do that, I would not be allowing Jesus to draw people to His heart through my story! It is not about me; it has never been about me. It has always been about loving God, loving others, and making disciples. God didn't cause anything to happen to me, but He brought me out of so many areas of life, especially the homosexual lifestyle, because He wants me to spread His message!

The main fear that Christians have when facing this area of life is rooted in a major misconception. The misconception is that they will not be able to relate to those who are different from them. They believe that everyone they talk to will hate them or think they are judging them. This is sometimes true, but mostly because homophobic people have given the Church as a whole a bad reputation. However, that is all the more reason to go repair the wound that was created! When it is a sin that Christians deem as very small, they are willing to tell someone that they're sinning. For example, it is easy to tell someone they are being prideful or that they're gossiping too much. However, when it comes to homosexuality, for some reason, we've taken it into its own category. We are so scared of it. It is time to end that!

God never put it in a separate category. God never saw it as worse than anything else in the Bible. God categorized it with all other sins, and God never calls us by our sin! Jesus Christ died so that we would not have to be known by our sin; Jesus paid the price for our sin. It is finished! That is why we cannot afford to continue believing that and acting like homosexuality is a huge thing! I am so thankful for people who saw me as a daughter of the one true King and loved me unconditionally. When people at the church welcomed me in with open arms, it showed me what true unconditional love looked like. The love I had always been searching for didn't come from a romantic relationship. The love of God was overflowing out to me through them. The world seeks that kind of love on a daily basis, but it never finds it.

If you know what the love of Jesus feels like—and if Jesus has redeemed you and saved you from anything in your life—then you are fully equipped to help someone dealing with homosexuality. If you haven't dealt with homosexuality yourself or you don't know how to talk about it, no problem! You don't need to tell them that you understand what they're going through because in reality, you don't. You just need to understand that what they're going through is hard, it does not make sense, and it may even seem impossible to overcome.

We have all been there, and regardless of what someone is going through, they just need us to come alongside them and lovingly explain that we believe in a God of miracles and a God of the impossible. If something does not seem possible, then watch out because that is where God wants to come in and radically change things. They need someone to love them like Jesus loves them until they learn what Jesus's love really is and how to love themselves through it all.

In our world right now, there is an epidemic of identity crisis. The world is in an uproar, and people are believing that true freedom rests in the idea that they can be whoever they want to be. It's this concept of finding your own truth. Whether it's a different gender, whether it's their sexual orientation, or whatever it might look like for you, take note that finding your own truth is not being free-spirited. That is not true freedom. I want to set you free from the lie that freedom is being true to yourself. I want you to accept the power of a free Spirit, the Spirit of God, the Holy Spirit. I promise you will never imagine how your life can be transformed and changed into something so beautiful. It is way more powerful and way more satisfying. This isn't my promise to you; it is God's promise to you.

Ultimate freedom is accepting and receiving Jesus dying on the cross for our sins, saving us from darkness, rising again two days later, defeating death, and then ascending into heaven so that we could have the gift of the Holy Spirit! When we accept Jesus into our lives, we have a supernatural God living inside of us. His presence, the Spirit of God—the same power that raised Jesus from the grave—lives inside of us.

Let's work together to lead everyone into the presence of the Holy Spirit, so the Spirit of God can transfigure their lives—not just convert them—and literally transform them into something beautiful! When God changes them from caterpillars into beautiful, vibrant butterflies, people will naturally have the desire and the power to live out the will of the Holy Spirit.

How do we help people understand this? Well, we need hope. We need faith. We need positivity! Unfortunately, a lot of churches and Christians lack hope. When many of them approach people who are trying to work through homosexuality, they do not know how to speak life and healing over them. I used to be neighbors with a guy who was dealing with homosexuality, and one evening, my husband and I joined him and his parents for dinner. His parents were heartbroken that their son might never be able to find love or intimate companionship. We could see it was a real fear in his heart as well.

This broke my heart, and it really fueled a fire in me. That is not God's heart. I told him that God would never hurt him and would not leave him there. God's heart is not to convert us, make us sit in our sin, and suppress our heart's desires. He would never make anyone have to deal with homosexuality on their own.

God wants us to sacrifice the things we believe are more important to us than He is. He calls us to lay ourselves down in front of Him and strip ourselves of all our identity so that He can give us our rightful identity in Him, an abundant life full of what our hearts desire, and even more than we can imagine on our own. Our human brains can't comprehend how much God is actually capable of and how much He can radically transform our lives. Once we step out of fear and into God's love, He can begin to really show us the true desires of our hearts.

If your desire is to find love, the Lord will provide that for you. It is going to look different than what you are imagining in your head. It takes a lot of faith and a lot of obedience. On the other side of faith and obedience is reward! You do not have to fear anything in this world because the Holy Trinity is far beyond your understanding. You have to trust in God. You have to trust in something much bigger than you: His mercy, His grace, His goodness, His kindness, and His love. They will provide the most amazing life for you.

I understood what that guy was saying, and it broke my heart. I related to him because I had been there before. I cried hard, almost every day, for about a year after I gave my life to Jesus because I thought I was never going to love again. I thought I was never going to have a family. I thought I was never going to know the feeling of having someone to take care of me. When I realized that those were all lies, Jesus came over me with an overwhelming peace that I didn't deserve or understand. I was suddenly content with the truth that Jesus was enough for me. I didn't need anyone else to fulfill me because God was enough.

As I became completely content with being single for the rest of my life, God started to answer my heart's desire. He blessed me with my husband. However, while my husband and I were engaged, I was so scared. We were willingly abstaining from all physical affection until we were married, and I had no idea what was going to happen. I had not been physical with a guy in a long time; when I thought back to the days where I was physical with men, I remembered that I never really enjoyed it. I was nervous.

I cried in fear almost every night. I did not know if I would be attracted to my own husband. I covered it with prayer, and God surely had other plans. My fears were real, but God was bigger. After our wedding day, we had sex for the first time—and my mind was blown. It was mind-blowing sex. God had restored my sexuality. I have never had more intimate and spectacular sex than with my husband. It just keeps on getting better too!

This is a great example of why we can't let our fears win. We cannot underestimate the power of God. Jesus does a mighty work when we empty ourselves for Him to fill us up. When they ran out of wine at the wedding in Cana, Jesus filled the need. He fills us when we run out. He filled me when I had nothing left. He continues to fill me every day. He fills me through His Word, through prayer, through fasting, and through His people.

There are battles that I have to face every day that I wish I did not have to. I opened a lot of doors that never should have been opened. I know what drugs feel like, what homosexuality feels like, and basically what fake satisfaction feels like. My mind will always try to bring those feelings back—and Satan will definitely try too—but God's power and goodness far surpass any of those trials. He helps me put on His armor and dive in headfirst to defeat giants. With God, all things really are possible. It's true! Never limit the power of the Holy Spirit.

A moment in the presence of God can cause change far greater than ever imagined. It causes a reaction in our bodies and in our hearts that can literally change our lives and the world in an instant. The Holy Spirit is the greatest gift to us. When Jesus rose from the dead and then ascended into heaven, He did it so that we could live with the Holy Spirit. Once we accept Jesus into our lives, we literally are living with God inside of us. It is unfortunate that so many people believe things are just the way they are, that some change is possible, but that miracles like this can't happen. That's what happens when we are only preaching about God and Jesus, but leave out the Spirit of God. People need to be aware that the Spirit that was hovering the earth before anything was created now lives in us believers! The church needs to speak about this more, and Christians need to come alive! Never limit the power of the Holy Spirit. Come alive, church!

We need to help people understand how to get filled up by the Spirit and not this world. We need to fight against injustice and stop sitting back while our world is enslaved! It is crucial for us to step in and show people living in this world what true freedom looks like! We need to love everyone, and we need to take action.

We do not have to support things that oppose God, but we do have to love everyone and speak truth into their lives. It is not love to omit what God is telling you to say to someone or to not love one another. My whole life, it was not like I believed in nothing. I knew there was some sort of God.

Since I was lucky enough to grow up in a church environment, that was the God I ended up turning to in the end. Many people are not being raised with knowledge of God anymore, and we need to help share the truth now more than ever! The truth will set you free, and we need to understand that the truth is not our truth; it's God's truth.

During these final pages, let's dive into what the truth really is. I always wanted to be attracted to men. I always wanted to have a family. I wanted to have kids. I viewed all of that as impossible. I deemed myself unworthy of it all. For the longest time, I acted like my dreams weren't there. I had convinced myself that I did not want those things in an attempt to make myself feel better. Something inside of me was so insecure and scared that no man would ever want me because I wasn't feminine enough, I wasn't pretty enough, and I wasn't good enough for him.

Once I began being rejected by guys in real life, Satan's lies took a deeper and greater hold in my mind. The lies literally pushed me to go out and seek women. What ended up happening was that one of my first and greatest God given dreams, that of having a family and being attracted to a godly man, was now something I was completely working against. I threw it aside and ignored it, and after ignoring something for a while, you stop believing in it.

If you are someone who has suppressed your dreams because you did not feel good enough to receive them, please know that you are! God has made you more than enough. You may be dealing with secret thoughts about your sexual identity or have already come out in a homosexual lifestyle. If you're a girl, you don't have to wear makeup, gossip, or like shopping. You don't have to be like all the girls on *The Bachelor,* which was a show that, for me, always fed my own insecurities. You don't have to like things that society has deemed feminine. If you're a boy, you don't have to like football, play sports, or like cars. You can just be you! God wants you to be true to who you are, according to His will for you. You're allowed to be creative! God never said that we have to fit the societal mold. He just told us that actively living a homosexual lifestyle is sin.

The good news is that God does not want to change who He designed you to be. Girls, you are allowed to play sports! Guys, you're allowed to go shopping! I cannot reiterate it enough that your personality does not equal your sexuality. Gender is given to you before you are born; you come out male or female. God designs us before we even exist. There is no denying that, but your hobbies and your personality have no relation to your gender. There is freedom when you accept who God has designed you to be and stop letting the culture and world define you! That is real freedom. I know because I am finally living in it.

Be who God has called you to be because the only focus should be on Jesus! The focus is to become more like Jesus—not more like a boy or a girl. My whole life was built around the pressure of fitting in and becoming someone I was not. Why would I want a religion that is based on a God who forces me to be someone I am not? The answer is so clear! God will never force you to become anyone you are not. When you submit your life to Christ and fall madly in love with Him, just watch as your entire life changes. No force—just love. You don't need to focus on trying to be someone you're not because God actually calls you to be who you are! God is love, and He believes that He created you perfectly and uniquely!

True freedom lies with God. When we focus on God, we are so excited and proud of the freedom we find! We need to focus on the things above and not the things of this world! We cannot allow the world and Satan to define us by our sin any longer. God ultimately wants us to be who He created us to be. He wants us to be who we truly are!

God is for you. He is not against you! You may have been in a church setting where people claimed or acted like God was against certain groups, but God is not against anyone. He loves you just the way you are—right where you are! He doesn't want us to fit in with the world. He wants us to stand out! He doesn't want us to be perfect, but he does want us to obey his guidelines and obey what He says is the right way to do life. This concept becomes easy to understand when we start loving Jesus and thanking Him endlessly for this life we get to live.

As far as guidelines and obedience go, we have to believe in wrong and right at some point. Our culture has adopted the idea that there is no right and wrong. We have lost respect for authority and laws. We are all running around in utter chaos with no structure. Some things are gray, but a lot of things are black and white. We cannot have a viewpoint that is only black and white; we also cannot have a viewpoint that's only gray! There is black and white, but there is also gray. What does God tell us about that? We need the Holy Spirit to guide us with His wisdom and knowledge. Without the Holy Spirit to help us understand the Bible, it is just a bunch of pages with words. We need the presence of the Holy Spirit right now, more than ever!

How can you lean in to the understanding of the Holy Spirit and ask Him questions? God wants to reveal his wisdom to you. God wants you to gain the wisdom and knowledge of Christ! First fear God. Honor Him and love Him more than anything or anyone else. Look to God for what is right and wrong. Stop looking at culture to tell you what is right and wrong! We cannot afford to continue to be slaves to culture. We need to obey God and not the world.

As a church body, we need the Holy Spirit's wisdom to navigate all the areas talked about in this book. At every point in my life, I realized that many people around me did not know how to talk to me. People said nothing or gave me unsolicited advice. Can I be real for a second? Almost no one wants advice from you—unless they are asking you for it. What is the best way to help others who are dealing with things like abuse, addiction, homosexuality, or mental illness? Your presence. Your presence, led by God's presence, is all that is needed. Come alongside them, comfort them, and pray with them. Simply love them. Ask God to help you see them as He sees them and to love them as God loves them. Take God's lead.

Many Christians say, "Well, if they believe that they are never going to change, and it is just who they are, then how am I going to change them? What do I do?"

Start by praying to get it in order because you are out of order. Your job as a saint is not to try to change anyone. That is God's business, and we have no place interfering with God. Regroup, speak life over them, lead them into the presence of God, love them, and speak the truth over them. Do not shove the truth in their face. Take it one step at a time, and when it is appropriate, pray all the fear away and speak the truth in love.

Maybe you are saying, "Chloe, I can't change. It is impossible."

So many people told me that I was going to continue struggling with the same feelings. They said I was still going to be gay and that I would just be suppressing it. First of all, God doesn't love you any less if you're gay. Secondly, temptation in and of itself is not a sin; sin is giving *into* the temptation whether it's in thought or deed. For a while, I actually did just suppress my sinful desires and tendencies. During that time, I was so desperate for God to fully heal me in that area. Then I received full healing. Many people do not know this part of my story.

There came a time where God wanted to show me how freeing

full healing feels. When my husband and I were engaged, I told him that I felt like I needed to go see my ex-girlfriend. I did not know why, but I felt like God was telling me to go. My husband is awesome, and with no questions asked, he told me to go. When I got to the meeting spot, I saw the only girl who could ever make me feel romantic feelings like that again. I looked at her and saw nothing. I felt nothing. It was like I was just sitting and talking with a best friend. It was the first moment when I knew that God had healed me and set me free into a new life.

God offers us full healings of many types and full miracles. Miracles happen in all different ways and at all different times. Never compare your miracle to someone else's and become defeated. I believe in a God of the impossible. I do not just believe because other people have asked me to. I believe because I have experienced it in my own life! Yes, it does take adjusting, and people often ask, "How do you do it?" The answer is love. I just prayed that God would cover me in His love.

To this day, I do not have all the answers. Only God is all-knowing. I invite His grace, kindness, and love into my life to overwhelm me each new day. It can surpass all negativity and all the bad desires in my life. To this day, I am not sure if God ever made me *straight* because I do not think God ever created the labels of *gay* or *straight*. All I know is that God's grace covered me and relieved me of the oppression I was facing under sin. He renewed my mind and together, in a beautiful partnership, we created new ways of thinking and new neural pathways. And then, one day, before I knew it, I had fallen in love with my husband.

I can't promise you that it won't be hard; it was hard for me, and every day brings its own battle. Like I said, where God is, Satan is following right behind trying to distract us. Nothing is more worth the fight. I get to wake up and look into the eyes of a tangible miracle from heaven every day. Whatever your heart's true desires are, if they are according to God's will, then God will bless you—and you will receive them. That is not my opinion. These are Jesus's words:

> Let us not become weary in doing good, for at the proper time we will reap a harvest if we do not give up. (Galatians 6:9 NIV)

> So I say to you: "Ask and it will be given to you; seek and you will find; knock and the door will be opened to you." (Luke 11:9 NIV)

Speaking of distractions and adversity, when I started walking with Jesus, a lot of people who identified as gay would come up to me and tell me that I was lying to myself. They would say that I was definitely gay and that I would find out one way or another. All of those people were gay, and truth be told, they were really trying to convince me to not follow Jesus. Spiritual warfare is so real. Each of them had been shunned from the church and hated for their same-sex attraction. They felt abandoned and hurt by the church. They felt like God wasn't real because if He was real, they would have felt loved and not hated. I think they were actually trying to protect me.

All saints need to change our approach. We need to understand the love of Jesus, and we need to invite these people back to church with us. We cannot just let them walk away because the church has hurt them. We need to find the people who have been wrongfully hurt by the church, and we need to apologize for what those people did to them. We need to represent the love of Christ and pray that the Holy Spirit will mend those wounds. Maybe church is too much right away. Maybe try grabbing some coffee and getting to know them.

A lot of people in the LGBTQ community have been hurt in one way or another by the church. Even if it was just by one Christian, we have to understand that we all represent the church. That is why I am emphasizing that our communication line between the two needs to be rebuilt. It is such a necessary topic to discuss and to learn about. We need to go out and redeem those relationships so that we can rectify them. Let us revive Christianity in a culture that thinks that Christianity has no place in it. I pray that the church becomes filled with people with same-sex attraction and gender confusion. I think it's about time we started respecting and honoring a group of people that used to be turned away from God's love. Honor and support are two different things; everyone deserves to be honored as a creation of God.

Maybe you are practicing homosexuality and do not like anything I am saying. This doesn't sound good to you? Okay, well, for years, I hated Thai food. Anytime someone wanted to get Thai food, I would think they were so weird. I would even debate our friendship and then just say no. The truth was that I had never even tried it. Now, my husband and I go all the time. It is one of my favorite types of food. It's the same with country music. I hated it. When I started listening to it, little by little, I understood it and came to love it. I go to Stagecoach and other festivals and have the best time of my life.

What am I getting at? You might hate Christianity, but do you really know anything about God? Do you understand who He is? Have you ever taken a look at what the Bible actually says versus what people around you have said about it? It is time to give God a chance. Don't let negative experiences with the church alter your progress now. You never know what you are missing until you get out there and give it a shot. I had to remove everything I heard my friends saying about God and church, remove everything I thought religion was like, and just go into it with an open heart and an open mind.

Maybe you were in the church but were hurt by the church. When I was in West Hollywood, I hung out with some big-name LGBTQ activists. The main thing I heard was that they actually grew up in the church, but the church made them leave. If you have been hurt by the church, I am sorry. I want you to know that Jesus loves you and that I love you. God is calling you back into His arms. He has been chasing you down, and it is time for you to answer His call.

God has so much planned for you. He has bigger plans for you than whatever is going on in your life right now. I know that His heart wants to see you in heaven. His heart wants you to join Him in this crazy journey of life and help lead others to Christ. There's a message inside your mess right now. There's a reason why you're in the place you're in. There's a reason why you're living out the things you're living out. There's a reason for everything, and God will use everything for good. He will literally take what the devil wants to be used for evil, and He will turn it into something beautiful—something far beyond your wildest dreams! You can change the world in the way that you have always wanted to.

If you are practicing homosexuality or dealing with a confusing spirit, I want you to know that that spirit is not the Holy Spirit. I pray that those spirits leave you right now, as you read this. God is a God of clarity. He provides clarity, and He can help you. His Spirit is not confusing. His Spirit is peace and understanding. I encourage you to start praying in the name of the Father, the Son, and the Holy Spirit. Start seeking out Jesus Christ—and trust in your heart that God wants you to succeed. Believe in Him and believe that He is your helper. God is for you. He's not against you. The one and only true God is not a condemning God. He is not a hateful God. He loves you just the way you are. He loves you with that sexual orientation. He loves you with that gender identity. He loves you. He is inviting you into a relationship with Him, and He is offering you a position as an heir to His throne. He is inviting you to inherit the kingdom of God and all the rewards and promises on this earth. Everything that belongs to Him can belong to you.

Maybe you are thinking, *Chloe, this sounds like a nice idea, but my life is good. I am good.* For my entire life, anyone else would've seen my life as something good. I had money, friends, relationships, an oceanfront apartment, a good job, and a good family. You name it! I was so good at acting like I had it all together on the outside because externally my life was going well! I actually believed it was going well too! Social media makes it so easy to post photos and create a life that looks so good—even when you are broken on the inside. I was the only one who really knew that I was alone and scared, but I was shut off from those emotions. I was the only one who knew I was missing something.

Maybe you are thinking, *Chloe, your story is pretty bad. My life* that you are, but the moment that we all start looking past our differences, stop fighting each other, and accept God as the Maker of this world, we will find pure freedom and pure unity. We have more in common than we don't. Let's love and not hate. I have never seen Jesus change a life through a hateful Christian. God can restore any relationship that's been hurt in the past, and God can restore a lost and broken world today! Don't forget that the battle has already been won. Jesus already defeated the grave. I am so thankful that we serve a God who is alive and who actually brings people together. God can take people's differences and use them in unique ways to change the world! God can make beauty from ashes and literally make anything out of nothing. I am so thankful that we serve a God who loves us too much to ever leave us or forsake us. God believes in marriage, family, and unity.

We also need to understand that a lot of people—way more than we think—are being raised without a concept of God. They have no church. They have nothing. We need to be careful and prayerful about how we talk to them about Jesus. A lot of people believe in a higher power, but they refuse to believe in Jesus.

When I was going through a lot of my battles, I went to Alcoholics Anonymous for a while. I made some amazing friends, and they knew that there was a higher power—and that was why they were able to be sober and receive healing. Many of those people said they were praying to a god, but it was never the God of the universe, Jesus Christ. I could see their hearts longing for a deeper connection, but not knowing anything. They were just desiring a communion with something bigger than this world. We need to ask the Holy Spirit to fill us with love and compassion so that we can understand that they are living the best life that they know of. Being a loving and gentle-spirited person is crucial. We need to represent Christ and go out and show the world what freedom in Him truly looks like! We need to be set apart.

This is a movement. This is the start of a conversation. This is a movement for Christians to wake up, experience God, and start living with the Holy Spirit. This is a movement for Christians to step out and stop hiding and running away from darkness. This is a movement for Christians to go into the dark and scary places, change the world, and set captives free!

In a world that thinks it is thriving under division—without even knowing the damage that is being done—we need to put on the armor of God and step out to create unity. We need to be the bigger people. When the world is silencing us, we need to get louder. We need to gain wisdom in every area of life, especially the ones we know nothing about. We need to be on guard, ready to fight any battle or help resolve any problem that comes our way.

Maybe you need to come out of sin and into God's loving arms. Maybe you need to ask God to take away the hate you have for others and fill those areas with His love. Maybe you need to ask God for the courage to have conversations that you have never had before. Wherever you are today, start praying big! Declare unity! Declare freedom! Declare healing! Believe that you can fight whatever you are going through—and watch God change it! Watch God move your mountains. Watch God do the impossible. He is bigger than you think He is.

> It is for freedom that Christ has set us free. Stand firm, then, and do not let yourselves be burdened again by a yoke of slavery. (Galatians 5:1 NIV)

Afterword

If the Holy Spirit touched your life and touched your heart while reading this book, please find a local church and a solid community to create relationships in. Be vulnerable and find Spirit-led people with contagious and inspiring faith to lean on. First and foremost, please accept Christ into your life if you have not or if you have strayed away from the faith recently. It is never too late to welcome Him into your life.

Say this prayer out loud:

> Jesus, I believe that You are the God of all the heavens and the earth.
> Thank You for creating me and choosing me to live this life.
> I ask that You would forgive me for my sins,
> and help me to walk as the saint that You call me..
> I invite You into my life, as my Lord and Savior,
> and allow You to have Your way.
> Change me from the inside out. God, I surrender my ways and my life to You.

Once you accept Jesus into your life, God starts to show off. Fully surrender to Him and start watching miracles happen left and right. You have to go all in. Do not hold back one bit. God loves you, and He is so excited that you have answered His call to come home. Heaven is throwing a party right now.

If you are already walking with Christ, I pray that this book has given you knowledge and insights about areas you might not have experienced. I pray that you know more now and will be able to go out and not shy away from conversations that need to be had! This world is in a major identity crisis, and instead of stepping back, saints need to step in. No more complaining about all of the darkness and confusion; let's actually get in there and make a difference. No more waiting for someone else to do it or just waiting for the end-times. It is always good to wait in expectancy for heaven and that moment when we get to meet God, but since God is here now and living inside of you, let's bring heaven to earth. Come on!

We all know someone who could benefit from reading this book. Please share it with them! You never know what God can do. Thank you for reading this book and for joining me in this movement. This book is not the end; it is only the beginning. I can't wait to see what God has in store!

Printed in the United States
By Bookmasters